NATIVE TRIBES OF THE NORTH AND NORTHWEST COAST

Michael Johnson
& Jane Burkinshaw

WORLD ALMANAC® LIBRARY

Please visit our web site at: www.worldalmanaclibrary.com
For a free color catalog describing World Almanac® Library's list
of high-quality books and multimedia programs, call 1-800-848-2928 (USA)
or 1-800-387-3178 (Canada). World Almanac® Library's fax: (414) 332-3567.

Library of Congress Cataloging-in-Publication Data

Johnson, Michael, 1937 Apr. 22-
    Native tribes of the North and Northwest Coast / by Michael Johnson and Jane Burkinshaw.
      p. cm. — (Native tribes of North America)
    Summary: An introduction to the history, culture, and people of the many Indian tribes that inhabited the region from the Arctic through the northern interior of Canada to coastal Alaska, British Columbia, Washington, and Oregon.
    Includes bibliographical references and index.
    ISBN 0-8368-5611-2 (lib. bdg.)
    1. Indians of North America—Northwest Coast of North America—History—Juvenile literature. 2. Indians of North America—Northwest Coast of North America—Social life and customs—Juvenile literature. 3. Indians of North America—Canada, Northern—History—Juvenile literature. 4. Indians of North America—Canada, Northern—Social life and customs—Juvenile literature. [1. Indians of North America—Northwest Coast of North America . 2. Indians of North America—Canada, Northern.] I. Burkinshaw, Jane. II. Title.
    E78.N78J55   2004
    971.004'97—dc22
    2003060451

This North American edition first published in 2004 by
World Almanac® Library
330 West Olive Street, Suite 100
Milwaukee, WI 53212 USA

For Compendium Publishing
Contributors: Michael Johnson and Jane Burkinshaw
Editor: Michael Burke
Picture research: Michael Johnson, Jane Burkinshaw, and Simon Forty
Design: Tony Stocks/Compendium Design
Maps: Mark Franklin

World Almanac® Library editor: Barbara Kiely Miller
World Almanac® Library graphic designer: Steve Schraenkler

Picture credits
All artwork (other than maps) reproduced by kind permission of Richard Hook. All photographs are by Michael Johnson or supplied from his collection unless credited otherwise below. Particular thanks are due to the staff of Royal Albert Memorial Museum and Art Gallery, Exeter, Devon, U.K., for assistance and access to its exhibits, archives, and excellent collections. Much of the material in this book appeared as part of *The Encyclopedia of Native Tribes of North America* by M. J. Johnson and R. Hook, published by Compendium Publishing Ltd. in 2001.

Cambridge University Museum of Archaeology and Anthropology, U.K.: pp. 37, 47; Royal Albert Memorial Museum and Art Gallery: pp. 1, 4, 5 (both), 14, 19, 20, 22, 23, 26 (below), 27 (above), 28 (below), 29, 32, 34, 36, 39 (below), 49 (both), 50 (above), 52, 53 (both), 54, 55, 56, 57.

Printed in the United States of America

1 2 3 4 5 6 7 8 9 08 07 06 05 04

Cover: Nuxalk (Bella Coola) dancers performing an excerpt from the winter ceremonial cycle in Berlin, c. 1885.

Previous Page: This pair of Inuit dolls is in the collection of the Royal Albert Memorial Museum and Art Gallery, Exeter, U.K.

Contents

Introduction   4

Tribal Names   11

Peoples of the North and Northwest Coast   12

  Athabascan   12

  Chinook   21

  Cree   24

  Haida   27

  Inuit (Eskimo)   29

  Kwakiutl and Kwakwaka'wakw   36

  Nuu-chah-nulth (Nootka)   38

  Ojibwa (Northern)   40

  Salish (Coast)   42

  Tlingit   48

  Tsimshian   50

  Other Tribes   51

Glossary   58

Museums   59

Further Reading   59

Index of Tribes   60

Introduction

For thousands of years, the people known today as Native Americans or American Indians have inhabited the whole of the Americas, from Alaska to the southernmost tip of South America. Most scholars and anthropologists think that the ancestors of Native peoples came to the Americas from Asia over a land mass connecting Siberia and Alaska. These first Americans may have arrived as long as 30,000 years ago, although most historians estimate that this migration took place 15,000 years ago.

According to this theory, Paleo-Indians (*paleo*, from a Greek word meaning "ancient") migrated over many years down through an ice-free corridor in North America, spreading out from west to east and southward into Central and South America. In time, they inhabited the entire Western Hemisphere from north to south. Their descendants became the many diverse Native peoples encountered by European explorers and settlers.

"INDIANS" VS. "NATIVE AMERICANS"

Christopher Columbus is said to have "discovered" the Americas in 1492. But did he? Columbus was not the first European to visit what became known as the New World; Viking mariners had sailed to Greenland and Newfoundland almost five hundred years before and even founded short-lived colonies. Using the word "discovered" also ignores the fact that North America was already inhabited by Native civilizations whose ancestors had "discovered" the Americas for themselves.

When Columbus landed on an island he called San Salvador (Spanish for "Holy Savior"), he thought he had reached China or Japan. He had sailed west intending to get to the East—to Asia, or the fabled "Indies," as it was often called by Europeans of the time. Although he landed in the Bahamas, Columbus never really gave up on the idea that he had made it to the Indies. Thus when Native people first encountered Columbus and his men in the islands off Florida, the lost explorer called them "Indians." The original names that each tribal group had already given to themselves usually translate into English as "the people" or "human beings." Today, some Native people of North

America prefer to be called "American Indians," while others prefer "Native Americans." In this book, Native peoples will be referred to by their tribal names or, in more general cases, as Indians.

Today's Indians are descended from cultures of great historical depth, diversity, and complexity. Their ancient ancestors, the Paleo-Indians, developed beliefs and behavior patterns that enabled them to survive in unpredictable and often harsh environments. These early hunter-gatherers had a close relationship with the land and a sense of absolute and eternal belonging to it. To them, everything in their world—trees, mountains, rivers, sky, animals, rock formations—had "spirit power," which they respected and placated through prayers and rituals in order to ensure their survival. These beliefs evolved over time into a fascinating and diverse series of creation stories, trickster tales, songs, prayers, and rituals passed down to and practiced by tribes throughout North America. Although many Indians today practice Christianity and other religions as well, many of their traditional songs, stories, dances, and other practices survive on reservations and in areas where substantial tribal groups still live.

A CONTINENT OF CULTURES

Long before the Europeans arrived, important Indian cultures had already developed and disappeared. The ancient Adena and Hopewell people, for example, built a number of extraordinary burial mounds, and even large towns, some of whose remains can still be seen at sites in the Midwest and South. These cultures were themselves influenced by Mesoamerican (pre-Columbian Mexican and Central American) farming cultures based on growing maize (Indian corn), beans, and squash. They became the Mississippian culture from 700 A.D. The spread of language groups across the continent also points to a rich Indian history of continual movement, invasion, migration, and conquest that took place long before European contact.

By the time the first Europeans set foot in North America, Indians had settled across the vast continent into different tribal groups and cultures that were active, energetic, and continually changing. American Indians were skilled in exploiting their particular environments in a multitude of ways developed over time. They were also

Left and Below: Ilchinik—a totem pole by Nuu-chah-nulth (Nootka) artist and carver Tim Paul (Below). He carved the totem pole at the Royal Albert Memorial Museum and Art Gallery in Exeter, UK, in 1998. He was assisted by a team that included Patrick Amos (Bottom).

This red cedar pole is named for a successful and powerful whaler. He is seen at the base, in a state of trance, preparing himself for a hunt. He stands upon a whale, enclosed by the sides of the canoe. Also depicted are Tu-tu-ch, the elder Thunderbird; Ti-as, the New Moon; and the chief's box, Hu-pa-kwa-num. The face of the sea chief, Ha-witiisum, is on the lid of the box.

POTLATCH

The most distinctive feature of Northwest Coast culture is the *potlatch*. From the Nuu-chah-nulth *patshatl*, meaning "to give," this ceremony includes speeches, songs, dances, feasting, and gift distribution. Although these occasions once lasted for several days, a modern potlatch is unlikely to extend longer than a weekend.

The formal potlatch was held to enhance and confirm the host's elevated status within the society, and to legalize his claims to a noble title. In the past, potlatches were held to celebrate births or marriages, or to proclaim a daughter's first menstrual period. Others occurred upon the death of a leader, to mark the raising of a totem pole for prestige purposes, or to honor a deceased chief. They are held today for births, namings, weddings, anniversaries, graduations, special birthdays, and as memorials for the dead.

Invited guests, who may number in the hundreds, show approval of the host's claims by accepting payment in the form of food and goods. In the nineteenth century, the First Nations' wealth increased from contact and trade with Europeans—especially via the fur trade with the Hudson's Bay Company. Wealth display and gift giving at potlatches, therefore, could reach ostentatious heights. Nowadays gifts are more modest, although each potlatch can still cost a family or clan thousands of dollars.

good at incorporating new methods and technologies from other peoples. When Europeans came, many Indians adapted the newcomers' technology to their own way of life, incorporating, for example, the horse, the rifle, money, beads, fabric, steel implements, and European-style agriculture into their own traditional cultures. In many cases, however, the benefits of European influence were eventually overshadowed by the displacement or outright destruction of traditional Native life.

WHAT THIS BOOK COVERS

The purpose of this book is to give some relevant facts about each of the main tribes native to the Arctic, the Subarctic, and the Northwest Coast of North America. Included here are brief historical sketches of the tribes, descriptions of their language relationships and groups, and accounts of traditional cultures, locations, and populations in early and recent times. Interaction with invading Europeans is shown in discussions of trade, wars, treaties, and the eventual Indian removal to lands whose boundaries served more to keep Indians in than to keep white settlers out. Today's political boundaries were not recognized by Indians on their original lands; their "borders" were defined by shifting areas of hunting, gathering, and farming that Native groups used and fought over. For ease of reference, however, tribal locations given here refer to modern U.S. and Canadian place names.

THE TRIBES OF THE NORTHWEST COAST

The Northwest Coast culture area is a narrow strip of land between the interior mountains and the Pacific Ocean, relatively isolated from the rest of the North American continent. A mild and wet, heavily forested area, it extends along the Pacific coast from Yakutat Bay, Alaska, to northern California. This jagged mountainous coast is deeply notched with sounds, inlets, and fjords encompassing many islands, especially in the north.

The peaks of Northwest Coast culture were formed by the Haida-Tsimshian-Tlingit of the far north and the Kwakwaka'wakw (Southern Kwakiutl) of British Columbia with the Nuu-chah-nulth (Nootka) of Vancouver Island, each characterized by the highly developed art of carving wooden, red cedar totem poles, house fronts, masks, and

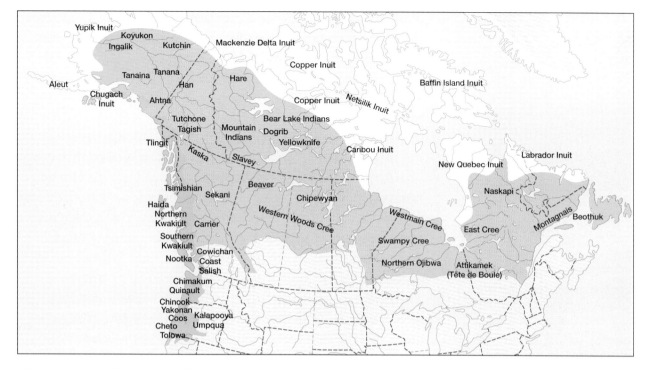

other ceremonial items; distinctive totem painting; and superb basketry. To the south, into Washington and Oregon, this distinctive culture is less strong—although the Coast Salish produced some carving and fine basketry, and the Chinook held occasional potlatch ceremonies.

TOTEM POLES

The art of carving and erecting large memorial columns—totem poles—though familiar to most of us as representative of Northwest Coast art, is probably not of ancient origin. Early European explorers do not seem to have noted them, so the acquisition of metal tools from non-Native traders may have given the Indians the means of developing their special techniques of massive wood carving. Before these totems had reached their imposing proportions, carving seems to have been used for grave posts, house fronts, masks, and stone objects of considerable antiquity. At some point carved poles became fashionable, with ambitious chiefs announcing their wealth and identity by commemorating their ancestors in wood. The spirits of these ancestors could be beautifully represented in animal, bird, or mythological forms—e.g., Eagle, Raven, Owl, Bear, Beaver, Wolf, Frog, Shark, Whale, Halibut, and Salmon—on ever more impressive poles.

To the south, the Chinook traded dried salmon,

Above: **The territory covered by this book divides into three distinct areas:**

- **white: the Arctic—the northern edge of the continent between Alaska and Greenland**
- **gray: the Subarctic—the northern interior of Canada and the interior of Alaska**
- **green: the Northwest Coast—coastal Alaska, British Columbia, Washington, and Oregon**

There is no record of the number of Indians living north of the Rio Grande before Europeans came. A conservative estimate of Indian population made by ethnographer James Mooney is about 1,250,000 for the late sixteenth century, before the founding of Jamestown and Plymouth. Others have suggested figures as high as six million, although two to three million might be more realistic. The highest concentrations of people were in the coastal regions: the Atlantic slope in the East, along the Gulf of Mexico in the South, and in California in the West. Indians living in these areas also suffered the most from European diseases and from conflict with European colonists. Population figures for the twentieth century vary considerably, due mainly to U.S. government criteria used to determine who is or is not an Indian. Also, the U.S. Bureau of Indian Affairs (BIA), the official bureaucracy in charge of the remaining Indian lands and federal services to Indians, has few relations with Indians in certain states. Thus the BIA's population figures tend to be lower than those reported by the U.S. Census. In 1950, the BIA reported 396,000 enrolled Indians, of whom 245,000 were resident on reservations. The U.S. Census reported 827,108 Indians in 1970 and 1,418,195 in 1980. Census 2000 recorded 2,409,578 respondents who reported as American Indian or Alaskan Native only and identified a single tribe of origin.

dentalium shells, and at times even slaves from California in return for material goods from farther north. Houses here were more simply made and for single families. In southern Oregon and northwestern California, redwood rather than cedar was the primary wood used. Deerskin robes and skirts replaced the woven cedar bark robes of the north. The southern peoples made fine basketry or imported it from California groups farther south.

Northwest Coast culture suffered a collapse in the late nineteenth century, when Indian populations were literally decimated by introduced diseases against which they had no immunity. In addition, Christian missionary influence and government plans for assimilation into white culture encouraged rejection of traditional cultural practices. The *potlatch*, the cornerstone of First Nations (a name for Canadian Indians) society, was outlawed in 1884. The anti-potlatch law was widely flouted, especially among the Kwakwaka'wakw (Southern Kwakiutl) and in the more remote regions of British Columbia. It remained on the statute books, however, until 1951. Items of ceremonial regalia confiscated during the time of potlatch banning have only been returned to their rightful owners during the last twenty-five years.

SUBARCTIC

The Subarctic is the whole of Quebec and Newfoundland, the northern parts of Ontario, Manitoba, Saskatchewan, and Alberta, the northern interior of British Columbia, the Yukon, the drainage of the Mackenzie River around Great Slave and Great Bear lakes, and the interior of Alaska. Except for the Beothuk, the Subarctic peoples are drawn from the Algonkian family in the east and the Athabascan family in the northwest. Within this vast area, culture remained constant, though flexible, with hunting and fishing the main means of subsistence. In this harsh climate, temperatures below –40°F (–40°C) are common in the long winters, but often reach 80°F (27°C) in summer, accompanied by a dense insect life which plagues humans and animals.

Much of the area is Arctic lowlands with abundant coniferous trees such as spruce, tamarack, willow, and alder. The topography ranges from forest to lake, swamp, prairie, tundra, mountain, and sea.

Animals of economic significance to the Native peoples of the Subarctic include moose, caribou, bear, fox, wolf, otter, and beaver. Important fish include whitefish, grayling, trout, and pike. A significant number of Athabascan groups lived in the great mountain chain of the Yukon Territory and British Columbia, in the lush river valleys of spruce, fir, cedar, and hemlock forests. Only at Cook Inlet, Alaska, were the people partly dependent upon the sea for food. Fishing also became more important at the close of the fur trade era.

Religion focused on the relationship between the animal spirits and man, and the spirits of natural elements such as fire, wind, and water. Shamans were important in helping to prevent disease and in enlisting the power of animals. Communal ceremonies were few, except where influenced by other cultures such as the Inuit or Northwest Coast peoples; western Athabascans' rich ceremonial life was partly derived from coastal cultures.

The network of white fur trading posts was influential beginning in the late eighteenth century. European goods gradually transformed clothing, housing, and settlement patterns, and missionary influence modified religion and produced some Christian-Native hybrid cults similar to those found elsewhere in North America. Artistically, floral beadwork on cloth largely replaced porcupine quillwork and painting on hide in the decoration of Native clothing.

ARCTIC

The Arctic peoples were once known by the collective term *Eskimo*, a name given them by non-Inuit people, widely thought to mean "raw meat eaters," although some researchers now believe it came from the Montagnais word for "snowshoes." In the 1970s, Eskimo groups in Canada and Greenland adopted the name *Inuit*, which means "we, the people." It has not been accepted in Alaska or Siberia. The Arctic cultural area, exclusively the home of the Inuit and the Aleut, extends in a 5,000-mile (8,000-kilometer) sweep from Siberia to Greenland, including most of the islands and coastal areas of Alaska, northern Canada (including Labrador), and Greenland. In this almost treeless land, the climate is so cold and the coasts lashed by such vicious storms that it seems outside the realm within which humans can survive, let alone flourish.

CENSUS 2000 FIGURES

Wherever possible U.S. Census 2000 figures are supplied with each entry showing the number of people who identified themselves as American Indian or Alaskan Native and members of only one tribe. Other people reported as American Indian or Alaskan Native in combination with one or more other races, or showing more than one tribe of origin, are identified as "part . . ." Reporting variables mean that some of the totals published here may not be the precise sum of the individual elements.

TERMINOLOGY

Throughout this volume the term "tribe" is often used interchangeably with "people," "peoples," "group," or "Nation." Although used frequently—and often acceptably—in the United States, "tribe" is more a bureaucratic or governmental term tied to treaty rights and the law. The U.S. government's acknowledgment of a Native group as a "tribe" gives that group access to government programs. In Canada, "Nation" is the preferred title except in a few cases, such as that of the Blood Tribe in Alberta.

Right: **Tribal names are—
for the most part—
not the old names
the Indians knew
themselves. Many
names translate simply
as "the real men" or
"original people." The
common, popular,
modern names used are
derived from various
sources. Some are from
Native terms, either
from the people for
themselves or names
applied by neighbors or
enemies, or corruptions
of these terms. Some
tribal names are
anglicized (made
English) forms of
translated Native names;
others are from French
or Spanish sources. We
use the tribal names
most commonly
encountered in history
and literature, although
it should be noted that
some modern Indian
groups have successfully
reintroduced their own
names into current
usage.**

Left: **A gift to Queen
Elizabeth II from British
Columbia, this totem
pole was carved by
Chief Mungo Martin
Kwakiutl and marked
the province's centennial
in 1958. The pole,
at over one hundred
feet (30 meters) high
and thirteen tons
(11.8 metric tons), is
made from western
red cedar and stands
in Windsor Great
Park, England.**

The Inuits' ancestors seem to have been the last major influx of people coming from Siberia across the Bering Strait, perhaps between 5000 and 6000 B.C. The Aleuts probably split from the main group early on. These first Inuit people probably reached modern Greenland in about 2000 B.C.; archaeologists have discovered there the remains of settlements they call the Dorset culture. Far to the west, along the coast of the Beaufort Sea, the remains of another early culture have been found, named Thule. It is believed that these people or their descendants swept rapidly eastward from about A.D. 800, settling along the ice-free shores of Greenland and absorbing the Dorset people. They also abandoned most of the northernmost Arctic islands, perhaps due to changes in the climate.

For their subsistence, the Inuit relied primarily on the sea and its large population of seals, whales, and walruses. In summer, when the landscape briefly became warm and sustained an abundance of plants and animals, they turned inland to hunt caribou, returning to the coast in fall and winter to fish and hunt sea mammals through blowholes in the ice. They survived mostly on fat and meat, much of which was eaten raw, giving them all the vitamin C required for health. With limited access to trees, the Inuits' tools, spears, harpoons, sleds, kayak frames, bows, and ceremonial masks often had to be pieced together in composite constructions from driftwood, antler, and bone.

Two groups, the Chugachigmiut or Chugach on Prince William Sound, Alaska, and the Kaniagmiut of Kodiak Island, were different from most Inuit. Both mummified their noble dead, built houses of wooden slabs that looked like those of the Tlingit on the Northwest Coast, and developed whale-hunting techniques similar to those of the Nuu-chah-nulth (Nootka) far to the south. Houses varied from the igloo of ice blocks among some Canadian Inuit to sod, wood, and whalebone semi-subterranean huts at winter village sites, and seal or caribou skin lodges during summer.

The Inuit remain superb sea and ice navigators, traveling by kayak, motorized boat, dogsled or snowmobile. Their world is filled with supernatural beings, usually interpreted by shamans. Infanticide was practiced and old people were left to die alone in times of great hardship, but exaggerated stories mask the Inuits' unique ability to survive in this harsh, cold, and dark environment.

TRIBAL NAMES

Tribe	Meaning of name	Tribe	Meaning of name
Ahtena	ice people	Nanaimo	bunch people
Aleut	island (possibly)	Nisqually	place name
Beothuk	human body	Nooksack	place of bracken roots
Cathlapotle	people of the Lewis River	Nootka	circling about
Cathlamet	village name	Nuxalk (Bella Coola)	English name
Chinook	village name	Puyallup	place name
Chehalis	village name (or sand)	Quileute	village name
Chetco	close to the mouth of the stream	Quinault	village name
Chilcotin	people of the river	Sekani	dwellers on the rocks
Chilula & Whilkut	people of the Bald Hills	Seechelt	place name
Chipewyan	pointed skins	Slavey	English name
Clallam	strong people	Snohomish	place name
Clatsop	dried salmon	Songish	name of local group
Comox	house	Squamish	people
Coquille	people who live on the stream	Stalo	upriver
Cowichan	warm the back	Suquamish	place name
Cowlitz	people of the river	Swinomish	place name
Cree	French version of own name	Tagish	place name
Duwamish	place name	Tahltan	place name
Haida	people	Takelma	those dwelling along the river
Han	those who dwell along the river	Tanaina	people
Hupa	place name	Tanana	Tanana River people
Inuit or Eskimo	people or raw meat eaters	Tête de Boule (Attikamek)	French—round heads (whitefish)
Kato	lake		
Koyukon	people of the river	Tillamook	place name
Kutchin	those who dwell on the flats	Tlingit	people or human beings
Kwakiutl	beach on the north side of river	Tsetsaut	those of the interior
Lassik	chief's name	Tsimshian	inside of the Skeena River
Lummi	facing each other	Tutchone	crow people
Makah	cape people	Twana	a portage
Mattole	place name	Umpqua	grass people
Montagnais–Nascapi	French—mountaineers	Wailaki	north language
Multnomah	those towards the water	Wasco	cup (or small bowl) of horn
		Yakonan	people of bay (or river)

The Aleuts were influenced by Europeans when Russian mariner-explorers settled on their islands and began the sea-otter fur trade; conversion to the Russian Orthodox Church followed. The Aleuts made fine waterproof clothing and excelled in basketry. They also used a two-man kayak or *baidarka*. Unlike the Inuit, they had a structured society of chiefs, commoners, and slaves.

The three major linguistic divisions of the Inuit are Aleut, the Yup'ik Inuit language (actually four to five languages, including Siberian), and Inupiaq. The Siberian Inuit may be people who resettled there from Alaska, or the descendants of the original people from whom all the Inuit originally split, or a mixture of both.

The Inuit population before European diseases was perhaps 60,000 and was reduced to half that by 1900. A recent estimate, including Greenland, shows a recovery to a figure in excess of their original population.

Names with no known meaning
Chastacosta, Chilluckittequaw, Chimakum, Clackamas, Clowwewalla, Coos, Dakubetede, Eyak, Hoh, Kalapuyan, Kaska, Kolchan, Muckleshoot, Nongatl, Ozette, Puntlatch, Queets, Samish, Semiahmoo, Siletz, Sinkyone, Skilloot, Skykomish, Snoqualmie, Squaxon, Taltushtuntude, Tolowa, Tututni, Upper & Lower Skagit, Watlala, Wishram.

English names
Bear Lake, Beaver, Bella Coola, Carrier, Dogrib, Hare, Ingalik, Mountain, Nicola, Yellowknife.

ATHABASCAN, ATHAPASCAN, or ATHAPASKAN

The Athabascan family is one of the most widely spread linguistic families of North American peoples. It has been tentatively allied with the Haida and Tlingit to form a larger generic group. The Athabascans are believed to be the last group, other than the Inuit, to enter North America from Asia via the Bering land bridge, perhaps between 5,000 B.C. and 8,000 B.C. They have for the most part occupied—in scattered groups—vast areas of Subarctic Alaska and northwest Canada beyond Hudson Bay. Perhaps 1,600 years ago, some Athabascans emigrated to the Pacific coast in southwestern Oregon and northern California. About 1,000 years later, a significant group entered the Southwest and became the Navajo and Apache.

Right: **Hupa White Deerskin Dancer, c. 1896. The Hupa, Yurok, and Karok had two major World Renewal rituals, correlating with the seasonal availability of major food resources: the Jumping Dance for the spring salmon run, and the Deerskin Dance for the fall acorn harvest and second salmon run. Performers held albino or other oddly colored deerskins aloft on poles, or carried obsidian blades covered with buckskin.**

WESTERN ATHABASCAN TRIBES

The Athabascan peoples arrived in the Northwest Coast area perhaps 1,000 years ago. The large territory held by the major communities of the Pacific Coast Athabascans extended not quite continuously from the Umpqua River in Oregon to the head of the Eel River in California. The California and Oregon groups each numbered about 7,000 in pre-contact times. Three small Athabascan groups are now extinct: the Nicola of British Columbia; the Kwalhioqua in the Willapa Hills of southwestern Washington; and the Clatskanie, who were likely Kwalhioqua who crossed into Oregon before 1775.

CHASTACOSTA

A group who lived on the lower course of the Illinois River near its junction with the Rogue River in southwest Oregon. They joined the general Indian resistance to white settlement, but were moved north to the Siletz Reservation where a few still live. They numbered 153 in 1858, 30 in 1937, and 20 in 1945.

CHETCO

These Athabascan people lived in wooden plank houses at the mouth of the Chetco River near Brookings, Oregon, and were closely allied with the Tolowa to the south. They aided other "Coast Rogue" groups in the general resistance of 1853–1856 and were moved north to the Siletz Reservation, where they numbered only 9 in 1910.

CHILULA and WHILKUT

Two small groups, almost indistinguishable from each other and from the Hupa. They lived in northwestern California, the Chilula on Redwood Creek west of the Hupa, and the Whilkut on the upper course of Redwood Creek and part of the Mad River to the southwest. The last of the Chilula moved to the Hupa Reservation and are no longer reported separately. The Whilkut suffered heavily at the hands of whites. Neither still exists as a distinct group.

COQUILLE

The Coquille lived in cedar plank houses on the east fork of the Coquille River, west of Myrtle Creek, in Oregon. They lived on acorns, deer, and fish. Some were forced onto the Siletz Reservation, where there were 15 "Upper Coquille" in 1910. A few dozen people of Coos-Coquille mixed descent known as the "Coquille tribe" live in the old location. The Coquille were one of many ancestries forming the "Confederated Tribes of Siletz," numbering about 900 shortly before the 1956 termination of their reservation. Siletz tribal rights were restored in 1977 and a new reservation established in 1979. In Census 2000, the number of Coquilles was 407 and the Tribes of Siletz totaled 2,707 including all respondents.

HUPA or HOOPA

Probably the largest and most important Athabascan group in California, living mainly on the Trinity River above its junction with the Klamath. They ate primarily salmon and acorns. Their elaborate "World Renewal" or "Big Time" rituals, involving ceremonials and wealth display, linked them culturally to the north. They lived in small villages of rectangular plank houses, wore buckskin aprons and skirts, and excelled in basketry. Extensive contacts with whites came after 1850, but the establishment of the Hupa Reservation helped maintain their numbers. Their population was over 1,000 in 1851; 420 in 1906; and 2,499 in 2000.

KATO or CAHTO

The southernmost Athabascan group of California, who lived in the upper drainage of the El River's south fork in Mendocino County. They originally numbered about 500, but in recent years only 95. All traces of their former culture have apparently disappeared.

MATTOLE

A small group who lived on northwestern California's Bear and Mattole Rivers, and a strip of adjacent coast. They perhaps numbered 1,000 in pre-contact times, but only 34 in 1910. In 1970, 30 of the "Bear River Band" lived at the Rohnerville Rancheria, Humboldt County. In 2000, there were 73, plus 27 Mattole.

Above: **A Northern Athabascan watch pocket, from the late nineteenth century, decorated with imported glass beads and silk ribbon—European-manufactured replacements for the indigenous materials of dyed moose and deer hair, bird and porcupine quill.**

SINKYONE

A group who lived mostly on the south fork of the Eel River to Shelter Cove on California's northwest coast. They have few descendants today.

TALTUSHTUNTUDE

These people, from the upper middle course of the Rogue River, Oregon, were subsequently moved to the Siletz Reservation. A group called "Galice Creek" numbered 42 in 1937, and 10 in 1945.

TOLOWA or SMITH RIVER

A group who occupied the Smith River drainage and some nearby coast in the northwestern corner of California. Linguistically they were closer to the Rogue River peoples to the north than to relatives to the south. They had permanent coastal villages of redwood plank dwellings in winter and moved inland for salmon and acorns in late summer. Ceremonies for the taking of the first salmon and sea lion link the Tolowa with the northern California "World Renewal" rites of the Karok, Yurok, and Hupa.

The overland explorations of mountain man Jedediah Smith were their first contacts with whites, and intensive white settlement of this region came after 1850. Probably numbering more than 1,000 in pre-contact times, disease and numerous attacks by whites reduced them to only 121 by 1910. In 1945, two small reserves, at Crescent City and Smith River, Del Norte County, reported Tolowa descendants as 37 and 113, respectively. In 1990, about 1,000 Tolowa, Tututni, and Chetco descendants were reported. In 2000, there were 960, including those who were part Tolowa.

TUTUTNI

A group of the Illinois and lower Rogue rivers in southwestern Oregon who also lived along the coast south to the Chetco River; they are commonly called "Coast Rogues." They were contacted by British explorer George Vancouver in 1792, and numbered about 1,300 by 1850. The Tututni suffered the same fate as many other southwestern Oregon groups, being shipped to the Siletz-Grand Ronde reservations in

1857. By 1910, only 383 survived; in 1930 just 41 were reported. In 1945, a few others under the names "Maguenodon" and "Joshua," numbering 39 and 45, respectively, seem to be of Tututni ancestry. They are now part of the "Confederated Siletz."

UMPQUA
Also known as "Upper Umpqua," they lived mostly on the south fork of Oregon's Umpqua River, near Roseburg, where they met Astoria fur traders in the early nineteenth century. They numbered some 400 by the mid-nineteenth century; forced north to the Grand Ronde Reservation, there were 84 in 1902. Descendants still live around Riddle south of Myrtle Creek. They were part of a reported 700 people in southwestern Oregon in 1956, descendants of Athabascans, Coos, Siuslaw, and others living around Roseburg and Coos Bay. The same group numbered 730 in 1970. By 2000, the Umpqua figure (including Cow Creek) was 736.

WAILAKI
Occupying the Eel River, south of the Lassik, to Big Bend Creek, they were culturally probably midway between the central California Wintu and their own northern relatives. In 1990, 1,090 Wailaki were reported from Round Valley Reservation; in 2000, 965.

NORTHERN ATHABASCAN TRIBES
The northern branch of the family comprises small groups, who occupied the Canadian and Alaskan Subarctic from the west coast of Hudson Bay to the interior of Alaska. In this vast area their culture was relatively uniform, without agriculture and primarily dependent on moose, caribou, or deer hunting. Houses were of bark or skins, modified into log houses during the late nineteenth century. Before trade goods became available, clothing was made from dressed skins. Vessels, toboggans, and canoes were built of wood, bark, sinew, and skins. When the fur trade arrived, guns, knives, and steel traps were adopted to hunt fur-bearing animals.

AHTENA
A group from the Copper River basin region of Alaska,

Above: **A Tolowa woman, c. 1890, wearing a classic two-piece skirt of the Klamath River area. Her narrow buckskin apron panel with clam and abalone shells covers a fiber and beaded skirt fringed with abalone "tinklers." Note the strings of shell beads and the basket hat.**

Below: **Northern Athabascan dog team, c. 1910. The dog team and its accoutrements were added to the Native flat-bottomed, hand-drawn toboggan by Europeans and Métis during the fur trade era, using European breeds stouter than the lightly-built, indigenous dogs. For deep snow and narrow trails, a toboggan was preferred to a runnered sled, with a team of four to eight dogs in a tandem hitch. A fully outfitted and adorned team had belts, tasseled and beaded blankets, and standing irons adorned with pompons. Sleds with raised runners and non-Native open sleighs were also used later in some areas.**

the Ahtena had few European contacts until about 1900. They still hold potlatches. Numbering perhaps over 500 at the time of Russian contact, they were reduced to some 300 by about 1900. Now they perhaps number about 500, including those of mixed descent.

BEAVER

These people, about 1,000 in pre-contact times, lived on the prairies and in the woods along Alberta's Peace River, northwest of Lesser Slave Lake. Among the first Northern Athabascans to experience European contact in 1792, they were gradually pushed westward by the gun-armed Cree. About 400 of their descendants, many also with Cree ancestry, live at the Boyer River reserves in Alberta; about the same number live in British Columbia. Census 2000 records 103 at Beaver Village.

CARRIER

A group inhabiting the upper Fraser River, British Columbia, particularly around Babine, Stuart, and François lakes. Their first European contact came with the Mackenzie expedition in 1793. In 1805, North West Company partner Simon Fraser established the first trading posts. The impact of traders, miners, and missionaries began to erode their culture by 1900. The Carriers depended upon fishing, collecting roots, and berries, and hunting beaver, goat, moose, and caribou. Their structures included wooden coastal-type houses, earth-covered lodges, and brush shelters. Their 1793 population was about 8,000, and it is over 5,000 today.

CHILCOTIN

A branch living on the Chilcotin River, central British Columbia, closely related to the Carrier. Their material culture included wooden rectangular and gabled houses, snowshoes, spruce bark and dugout canoes, fur blankets and robes, buckskin moccasins, aprons, and kilts. They fished and hunted elk, deer, caribou, mountain goat, and moose. The Chilcotin made coiled basketry with imbricated (overlapping like roof tiles) designs. Their present descendants number about 1,800 people—perhaps twice the ancient population.

EYAK
A small group on the southern coast of Alaska between Prince William Sound and the Tlingit of Yakutat Bay, near the mouth of the Copper River. Some still live at Eyak (Cordova) where the economy revolves around the fishing industry. Census 2000 reports 379 in the tribe. Some studies suggest that the Eyak may have Tlingit, Athabascan, Inuit, and even Asiatic ancestry, and that they should be treated as a separate linguistic family.

HAN
A small group on the Yukon River near the boundary between the Yukon Territory and Alaska. One of the last Athabascan groups to be contacted by whites, the Han's culture was effectively destroyed by missionary influence and the Gold Rush. Their descendants remained at Eagle and Moosehide, later Dawson, Yukon Territory, where about 300 still live.

INGALIK
A group living in the basins of the Yukon and Kuskokwim rivers, the most westerly Athabascans in Alaska. A northern division on the Innoko River, the Holikachuk, are sometimes now considered separately. Their ceremonial life seems to have been influenced by the Inuit, while their potlatches suggest Northwest Coast influences. The Russians established trade with the Ingalik during the early nineteenth century, modifying their culture and religion. A population estimate is 1,500 at contact, reduced to about 500 by 1900. In 1974, 530 Ingaliks were estimated at Holy Cross, Anvik, and Shageluk, some also of Inuit and white descent. In 2000, the total number of Alaska Athabascans in these villages was 251, while 54 Holikachuk descendants lived in Grayling.

KASKA
These people lived along the Liard River at Watson Lake, Yukon Territory, and the Dease River tributary. Closely related to the Tahltan and Tagish, they were

Below: **A museum model of a Northern Athabascan hunter wearing a leather beaded jacket, mittens, and pouch and holding a gun scabbard.**

Above: **Kutchin man,
c. 1862.** Northern Athabascan
men's summer dress was
characterized by a long-sleeved
pullover shirt with a distinctive
pointed lower edge, combined
moccasin-trousers, and mittens.
Usually made of caribou hide,
garments were decorated with
dentalium shells and porcupine
quillwork, the seams often
highlighted with red ocher.
After about 1850, Subarctic
clothing began to be greatly
modified in cut and materials
by European influences.

once collectively called Nahani. White contact began in
the 1820s with the establishment of a Hudson's Bay
post on the Liard, followed by increasing intrusion by
miners, traders, and trappers. In recent years, there
were 533 Kaska in the Liard River Band.

KOLCHAN
A group on the upper Kuskokwim River in Alaska,
sometimes considered a branch of the Ingalik but
related more closely to the Tanana. They have about
150 descendants at McGrath, Nikolai, and Takotna.

KOYUKON
Bands in three groups occupying the middle Yukon
River, Alaska, plus parts of the Koyukuk and Tanana
rivers. Contact with outsiders began in 1858 when the
trading post at Nulato was established by the Russian-
American Company. The Koyukon viewed the
supernatural world through animal spirits, and
held elaborate mortuary ceremonials and memorial
potlatches. Their religion has been modified over
the years from association with Roman Catholic
and Episcopalian missionaries. Their population was
perhaps 2,000 in pre-contact times; today about that
same number are reported in several villages.

KUTCHIN
One of the most important Athabascan branches,
scattered over an area extending from the middle
Yukon River in Alaska east into the Mackenzie River
drainage. Caribou provided food and clothing, but
freshwater fish and fowl were also important. Houses
were both surface and semi-subterranean log and
brush structures. The earliest known encounter with
Europeans was with fur trapper and explorer Alexander
Mackenzie and his men in 1789. The pre-contact
Kutchin numbered about 5,000, but fell below 1,000 in
1860. In recent years, 2,150 Kutchin were reported.

NICOLA
A designation of a small group of Athabascan-speaking
peoples in the Nicola and Similkameen valleys, British
Columbia, possibly of Chilcotin origin, though

culturally they are aligned with the Thompson with whom they have now apparently merged. Their language has been extinct since about 1910.

SEKANI
A people of the Finlay and Parsnip river valleys, both branches of the Peace River in north central British Columbia. Their language suggests a close relationship with the Beaver and Sarcee, and they may originally have been all one people. They hunted moose, caribou, mountain sheep, buffalo, and elk. Simon Fraser established two fur trading posts in their territory in the early nineteenth century. They suffered greatly from an influx of white miners beginning in 1861. They may have numbered 800 in early times, but only 160 were reported in 1923, 290 in 1934, 336 in 1949, and 523 in recent years. Many are thought to be of Métis descent. They now live mainly at Finlay River (Ware) and McLeod Lake, British Columbia.

TANANA
The name for several groups in three divisions along Alaska's Tanana River: the Lower Tanana near Fairbanks, the Tanacross around the town of the same name, and the Upper Tanana or Nabesna. Contact with non-Natives came first at the Lower Tanana, which was closest to the Yukon River trading posts in the early nineteenth century. The Tanana culture was modified by fur trade, missionary influence, and mining activities. Dependent upon caribou, other big game and fishing, their material culture included canoes, toboggans, skin boats, sleds, fish weirs, caribou-skin clothing, dyed porcupine quillwork, and beadwork on decorated festive clothing. Their population may have dropped to 700 in 1880 due to foreign diseases that continued well into the next century. About 600 descendants now live in Minto, Nenana, Tanacross, Tetlin, and Northway.

TANAINA
Groups living at Cook Inlet, Kenai Peninsula, and areas north and west in Alaska. Their culture was midway between those of the coastal Tlingit and the

MÉTIS
In Canada this word means a mixture of European, especially French, and Indian heritage, particularly those who settled around the Red River in present day Manitoba. Following rebellions against Britain, they scattered west to Alberta during the late nineteenth century. Omitted from treaties with Britain, the Métis together with non-treaty Indians (Indian women and their descendants who married non-Indians) form a large number of people across Canada who are today pressing for their own rights.

Below: **Cree or Cree-Métis moccasins collected at Hudson Bay and dating from the late nineteenth to the early twentieth century. The Hudson's Bay Company, originally set up to trade in the northern regions of the American continent as early as 1670, would have been the source of the silk floss and ribbon.**

Below: **A Tahltan-style shoulder bag from the late nineteenth century, made of cotton fabric with red trade cloth facing and a backing of green woven wool cloth. The front is beaded and tasseled. The strap is made of cotton and red trade cloths.**

interior Athabascans. Originally dependent on salmon, they also hunted moose and caribou. Contact with Russians in the late eighteenth century established their association with the fur trade and the Russian Orthodox Church. Epidemics during the nineteenth century reduced their population from 4,000 to 1,500. In recent years, about 530 Tanaina lived at Nondalton, Pedro Bay, Tyonek, Lime Village, and Eklutna.

TAGISH

A small but important group around Tagish Lake in southern Yukon Territory. Interaction with the Tlingit led the Tagish to adopt coastal traits such as the potlatch. Their culture was otherwise similar to that of other interior Athabascans. Their first direct contacts with whites were in the 1880s, but the 1898 Klondike Gold Rush brought major changes. About 200 descendants live at Carcross and Whitehorse, Yukon Territory, some probably part of the Inland Tlingit.

TAHLTAN

Centered on the upper basin of the Stikine River in northwestern British Columbia, the Tahltan, with the Kaska, Tagish, and Taku, were once referred to as Nahani. They hunted moose and caribou for meat and hides for clothing. They had extensive contacts with the coastal Tlingit and indirectly with the white fur trade. Direct European contact occurred after 1874. The pre-contact number was around 1,000, declining to less than 300 by 1900. Principally located on a reserve near Telegraph Creek, there were 702 in 1969.

TUTCHONE

Athabascans of southern Yukon Territory east of the Saint Elias Mountains. A mixture of tundra, boreal forest, and meadowlands supported moose, caribou, and mountain sheep which, together with salmon, provided their main food and clothing source. The Klondike Gold Rush and the building of the Alaska Highway changed native life. The Tutchone population was less than 1,000 in 1880. About the same number were reported in Yukon Territory, including some Tagish and others.

A small group inhabiting the lower Columbia River in Washington and Oregon upriver to The Dalles. The Chinooks were primarily a bay and river people, dependent on salmon fishing, as well as game. They lacked the developed wood-carving art of the northern coastal peoples. They have been divided into the Upper and Lower Chinook, referring to their locations on the Columbia. Their first non-Native contact was with Lewis and Clark in 1805, and afterward they were decimated by diseases brought by white traders. The majority of individual Chinook groups became extinct as separate identities before 1900; but a few hundred have fused with others on the Warm Springs, Yakima, Chehalis, Quinault, and Grand Ronde reservations in Washington and Oregon. The largest single element by 1950 were the Wasco at Warm Springs, Oregon. A few have lived off the reservations.

Before their population declined, the Chinook became the greatest traders on the Columbia, a great water highway from the coast into the immense interior. Their geographical position from the mouth of that river upstream made them middlemen in trade between the coast and the interior. The development of the Chinook Jargon, a trade language based originally on Chinook but later incorporating more European words, bears witness to the Chinook's importance in pre-1840 trade relations. Contacts and trade took place largely on the Columbia at Celilo or The Dalles, where material culture from the northern Plains mingled with and was exchanged for material from as far away as Alaska. From there the Nez Perce were the main outlet to the northern Plains via their associations with the Crow and the Flathead.

LOWER CHINOOK TRIBES

A group inhabiting the mouth of the Columbia River, giving their name also to groups in the interior. Their territory extended north to Shoalwater Bay, and they numbered 800 in 1800. They gained fame through

Below: **Head reshaping, c. 1846. Several Northwest Coast tribes, from the Nuxalk (Bella Coola) in the north to the Alsea in the south, reshaped the heads of babies, by the use of an additional wooden slat slanting downward from the top of the cradle and bound to the head or tied to the cradle base. The Chinook of the Columbia River valley practiced the most extreme flattening of the forehead. However, the so-called Flathead of western Montana did not follow this practice, leaving their heads flat on top.**

Above: **A Cree or Cree-Métis "octopus bag" collected before 1847. So named because of its eight tabs, this style of bag can be traced back to the late sixteenth century. Toward the end of the nineteenth century, octopus bags were also being made and used by the Tlingit and the Salishan-speaking nations on the Northwest Coast.**

CENSUS 2000

The numbers recorded for the Chinook were:

Chinook	611
Clatsop	17
Kathlamet	2
Wakiakum Chinook	2
Willapa Chinook	2
Wishram	1
Total	639

their trading, and the Chinook Jargon existed until 1900. From Lewis and Clark, November 1805: "This Chinook nation is about 400 souls, inhabit the country on the small river which runs into bay below us and on the ponds to the northwest of us, live principally on fish and roots, they are well armed with fusees and sometimes kill elk, deer, and fowl." Their few survivors mixed with the Chehalis or remained off reservations, and had almost disappeared as a separate people by 1945 when 120 "Upper Chinook" remained on the Quinault Reservation in Washington, including some descendants of the Chinook proper. Others have lived at the Shoalwater Bay and Chehalis reserves. In 1970, 609 "Chinook" were reported, excluding Wasco, apparently accounting for the whole family. Two smaller groups, the Wakiakum and Willapa, probably belong to this group.

CATHLAMET

A group forming a dialect division of the Chinook, who lived near the mouth of the Columbia River in Oregon and Washington to a point upriver near Rainier on the south bank. In 1806, Lewis and Clark estimated their population at 300. The explorers reported that the Cathlamet resembled the Killamucks, Clatsops, Chinooks, and Wac-ki-a-cums in dress, habits and manners. In Census 2000, only 2 were from this group.

CLATSOP

A coastal group of the Cape Adams area, Clatsop County, Oregon. With the survivors of the other ruined neighboring groups, they moved to the Grand Ronde Reservation, Oregon. Lewis and Clark estimated them at 300 in 1806; by 1910 they were reported as only 26. The Grand Ronde Reservation's general population was about 700 in 1955. In 1956, the reservation was terminated. It was reestablished in 1983, however, with additional land recovered in 1988. Restoration of the Grand Ronde economy includes gaming. In Census 2000, 17 full and 35 part Clatsop were reported.

UPPER CHINOOK TRIBES

CATHLAPOTLE
A Chinook group on the Lewis River in Clarke County, Washington, about 150 miles from the mouth of the Columbia River; now extinct.

CLACKAMAS
A division of the Chinook who gave their name to a dialect group. They apparently moved to the Grand Ronde Reservation, Oregon, and remained separate until recently. In 1945, 89 were reported, perhaps a combination of various Chinook tribal fragments.

CLOWWEWALLA
A Chinookan group of the Clackamas dialect, formerly living in Oregon on the Willamette River, a tributary of the Columbia. The Cushooks, Chahcowahs, Willamette-Tumwater, and others were divisions of this group, who for many years have been extinct as a separate people. The last Clowwewalla were said to be living on the Grand Ronde Reservation.

MULTNOMAH OR WAPPATO
A Chinookan group on Oregon's Sauvie Islands at the mouth of the Willamette River. Remaining members joined with related groups and lost their separate identity. They were closely related to the Clackamas.

SKILLOOT
A small Chinookan group at the junction of the Cowlitz and Columbia Rivers in Washington. At the time of Lewis and Clark (1806), they were living on both sides of the Columbia opposite the mouth of the Cowlitz and perhaps numbered 1,000. In 1850, they numbered about 200 and continued to diminish until they lost their separate identity. A number of nonreservation Indian descendants claim Skilloot ancestry.

WATLALA
A Chinookan group at the Cascades of the Columbia and Willamette rivers in Oregon. Survivors of the group joined the Wishram and Wasco and lost their separate identity. They are related to the Clackamas.

Above: **These bowls from the Wishram/Wasco region are made from mountain sheep horn. The Chinookian- and Salishan-speaking peoples of Washington's Columbia River area have a carving style characterized by formal surface decoration that differs from the figural imagery of the more northerly regions. These elaborately carved bowls, with their raised ends and designs of interlocking triangles, were used for ceremonial purposes. They were probably made in the late eighteenth to mid-nineteenth century.**

Below: **Swampy Cree woman, c. 1780. A few painted garments with dot, circle, and linear designs have survived in museums and are attributed to the Eastern and Swampy Cree of the Hudson Bay area before European styles and materials became influential. The rare side-fold dress, cape, hood, moccasins, and pouch display quilled and beaded ornamentation.**

The Kristinaux or Cree, an Algonkian people related to the Montagnais, Menominee, Sauk, Fox, Kickapoo, and Shawnee, are Canada's largest Native group. The term "Kristinaux" is either from the French word for "Christian" or from an Algonkian word meaning "first people." The Cree call themselves Ayisiniwok, meaning "true men," or Iyiniwok, Eenou, Iynu, or Eeyou, all meaning "the people." The Cree's importance was mainly due to the position they held in the Canadian fur trade and the influence this position gave them with other peoples. During the rearrangement of the Cree bands in western Canada, while they were involved with Hudson's Bay Company, the Cree were scattered over an immense area. No peoples in North America ever occupied as large an area as the Cree did at the height of their power. Although they were scattered so widely, there were only minor dialectical differences between most of the bands. Due to long separations, however, there were slight differences between the languages of the Plains and Woods Cree.

In short, before their historic westward expansion, the Cree were a typical eastern Subarctic people of Algonkian lineage. They can be generally subdivided into the West Main Cree, Woods Cree, and Plains Cree. There were probably Crees in the West before the advance of the fur trade, however, and an old group known as the Rocky Cree may have been in Saskatchewan before European contact. Missionaries organized a form of written syllabary of the Cree language which is still widely used. The total Cree population in 2000 was 2,488, with another 5,246 reporting partial Cree ancestry.

WEST MAIN CREE
This is the modern term covering the Cree bands formerly occupying the low-lying west coast of James Bay in northern Ontario, and formerly known as (or as part of) the Swampy Cree or Maskegon; and more specifically the Barren Ground, Fort Albany, Monsoni, and Kesagami Cree. European trading

posts in Swampy Cree territory were established in 1668 and 1671. Beginning in the late seventeenth century, these coastal Cree had adapted to the fur trade and Christian missionary teachings with a gradual modification to their Native culture. Besides being skillful hunters, they also fished. Both meat and fish were heat-dried to be preserved as winter food, often mixed with berries and animal grease. The Swampy Cree shared most of their religious beliefs with the Northern Ojibwa and Saulteaux. Their descendants live at Moose Factory, Fort Albany, Attawapiskat, Winisk, Severn, York Factory, Fox Lake, Shamattawa, and Churchill, Ontario, and numbered 6,345 in recent years.

WESTERN WOODS CREE

The Woods Cree are usually designated as the western extension of the Swampy Cree in Manitoba, Saskatchewan, and Alberta, Canada, during the later decades of the eighteenth century and the early nineteenth century. These Cree kept their basic northern forest culture, modified by their dependence upon the fur trade. They followed European traders and explorers deep into the north country, forcing the Chipewyans north and the Beaver Indians to the Rocky Mountains. Their material culture was largely replaced by European goods early on, but they retained snowshoes, toboggans, skin lodges, and bark canoes, plus some elements of their original dress such as moccasins. They excelled in decorative porcupine quillwork, painting, silkwork, and beadwork. Hudson's Bay Company was the economic authority of the whole region until the introduction of modern Canadian influences such as housing programs, health centers, and the developing micro-urban community. The Cree language, however, is still widely used.

The ancestors of the Swampy and Woods Crees

Above: **A pouch of black-dyed buckskin decorated with horizontal bands of woven porcupine quillwork in a style once common among the northern Great Lakes Indians but by the nineteenth century restricted to the Cree, Northern Ojibwa, and Athabascans of Canada. This pouch is probably of Cree origin, c. 1820.**

may have numbered 20,000 in the eighteenth century. In recent years, their population reached 35,550, exclusive of the Métis, in eight bands in Ontario (Constance Lake, Timagami, Matachewan, and others); fifteen bands in Manitoba (including Cross Lake, Fisher River, Gods Lake, Mathias Colomb, Nelson House, Norway House, Oxford House, and The Pas); nine bands in Saskatchewan (Lac la Ronge, Montreal Lake, and Peter Ballantyne being the largest); and thirteen bands in northern Alberta (Driftpile, Little Red River, Wabasca, Whitefish Lake, Sturgeon Lake, Fort Vermilion, and several others). In a number of locations, some Crees also have Northern Ojibwa and Saulteaux ancestry. For many years, Cree and Cree-Métis women have made moccasins, pouches, mittens, and jackets decorated with rich floralistic patterns in beads and silk and thread for sale or trade. Such items have been displayed in many museums in the United States, Canada, and Europe.

TÊTE DE BOULE OR ATTIKAMEK
A branch of the Cree who still live in the upper St. Maurice River region of Quebec, Canada, and who perhaps had contact with Europeans as early as 1630. Their general culture was similar to that of the Montagnais-Naskapi to the north and the Algonkin to the south. Although heavily influenced by the French-controlled fur trade, and subjected to Iroquois penetration, they continued to live independently until the introduction of Euro-Canadian industrialization in recent times.

Their Native dress seems to have disappeared early on, but they excelled in birch bark work and made excellent canoes. They presently have 3,000 descendants at Obedjiwan, Weymontachie, and Manouan in central Quebec; most still speak their Native language, and they are politically organized with their Montagnais neighbors.

Below: **A pair of nineteenth-century Eastern Woodlands snowshoes.**

The Haida were the original inhabitants of Haida Gwaii (the Queen Charlotte Islands), Canada and part of Prince of Wales Island in Alaska. They had the most spectacular Northwest Coast culture, with the finest and tallest totem poles. They lived in large community houses of heavy hand-hewn timber, decorated inside and out with carved and painted figures of massive proportions. The Haida are noted for their carvings in black

Far left: **A Cree warrior/hunter from the James and Hudson Bays area, c. 1815, clothed against the harsh climate.**

Below left: **Nineteenth-century European rather than traditional Haida images decorate this section of a ship-panel pipe. Depicted are a stylized tobacco leaf, two cascading bunches of tobacco berries, and a dancing sailor dressed in a frock coat. These pipes were not meant for smoking, but were carved as souvenir items.**

Below: **Haida village of Masset, Queen Charlotte Islands, British Columbia, and its totem poles. The pole on the far right is now in the Pitt Rivers Museum, Oxford, England.**

Above: **A Tlingit and Haida canoe. The southern Tlingit made canoes of red cedar, but all Tlingit preferred the great Haida canoes, up to 60 feet (18 m) long with masts and sails, which could carry several tons of freight. Such "war canoes" purchased by Tlingit chiefs bore their carved and painted crests at bow and stern.**

CENSUS 2000

The total for the Tlingit-Haida groups was 22,365, including 7,540 of partial descent. The largest elements are:

Haida	1,239
Tlingit	9,413

Below: **These Haida or Tsimshian spoons were painted in the northern style to represent salmon—one mouth open, the other closed. Collected before 1869.**

argillite, a carbon-rich shale found at Slatechuck quarry near Skidegate in Haida Gwaii. Strict control of this site ensures that all objects made from argillite are by Haida artists.

The first Europeans to reach the islands were probably Spanish explorers in 1774, followed by numerous traders, and finally by a Hudson's Bay Company trading post at Masset. The Haidas once numbered 8,000, but by 1895 the effect of smallpox, consumption, and alcohol had reduced them to 593 in Masset and Skidegate, Queen Charlotte Islands, and about the same number (known as Kaigani) at Kassan and Hydaburg on Prince of Wales Island, Alaska. In 1960, 391 Haidas lived in Alaska, and in 1970, 1,367 in Canada. In October 2003, the Haidas were successful in reclaiming the remains of 160 members from Chicago's Field Museum. Haidan is a Na-Dene language distantly related to Athabascan and Tlingit.

The Inuit constitute one complete linguistic family with the Aleut. They are usually considered separately from the rest of the peoples of North America, chiefly on physical grounds. Archaeological sites in the Arctic have been dated to between 2500 and 2000 B.C., and are designated as Independence I, Pre-Dorset, Dorset, and Thule cultures, the latter dating to approximately the thirteenth century A.D. All of these early peoples are direct ancestors of the Eskimoan people. They seem to have spread east and south to the Gulf of St. Lawrence, around the entire northern and northeastern coast of Canada, plus some parts of Greenland; along the coast of Hudson Bay, Baffin Island, and other northern islands; the coast of Alaska including Kodiak Island, and to the detached Chugach on Prince William Sound.

Despite a number of separate groups and a home territory of over 3,000 miles, the Inuit language varies sufficiently enough only to be classified into two divisions: the Pacific or Alaskan (Yup'ik) division, and the Canadian or Northern (Inupiaq) division. The settlement of the Inuit was as follows:

CENSUS 2000

Many Inuit/Eskimo groups were recorded in the census, the main groups of people being:

Eskimo	5,649
Inuit	534
Inupiat Eskimo	16,047
(including: 2,582 Inupiaq, 2,405.Inupiat, 1,255 Nana Inupiat	
Siberian Eskimo	1,381
Yup'ik	21,212
(including: 5,896 Yup'ik 1,800 Yup'ik Eskimo)	

BAFFIN ISLAND INUIT

The inhabitants of the eastern half of Baffin Island including the Nugumiut of Frobisher Bay, Akuliarmiut below Amadjuak Lake, Padlimiut on Home Bay, Qaumauangmiut on the Meta Incognita Peninsula, Akudnirmiut of Buchan Gulf, and Sikosuilarmiut of the Foxe Peninsula. Their present settlements are at Cape Dorset, Lake Harbor, Frobisher Bay, Broughton Island, Clyde River, and Pangnirtung.

Above: **An Inuit bone map representing a coastline, probably from the eastern Arctic region. Worn around the neck of a hunter seated in his kayak, it is a tactile as well as a visual image of sea mammal hunting and fishing areas. Collected before 1902.**

CARIBOU INUIT

Included a number of groups on Chesterfield Inlet, Baker Lake, and Thelon River almost to Churchill in northern Manitoba. Their present settlements are at Chesterfield Inlet, Baker Lake, Rankin Inlet, Whale Cove, and Eskimo Point.

Right: **Arctic kayaks. From top to bottom:**

Top: **A Caribou Eskimo kayak.** About 20 feet (6 meters) long and usually narrow, this decked, one-man hunting canoe was more widely employed than the umiak. The flat-bottomed or V-shaped frame of (usually driftwood) fir, pine, spruce, or willow is rigid without its (usually seal) skin covering—unlike bark canoes, which collapse on removal of the bark. The Inuit or Caribou Eskimos on the northwest side of Hudson Bay favored an extended prow and upraised stern-tilted cockpit and double-bladed paddles.

Center: **An Aleut** *baidarka*. About 25 feet (8 m) long, these craft have two or three cockpits and sharp sterns. The term *baidarka* has also come to be used in Alaska to designate Aleut or Inuit kayaks with forked bows. Provision was often made to hold a harpoon catch or trade goods on the deck, sometimes in a wooden frame.

Below: **A Western Alaskan kayak.** About 15 feet (5 m) long and noted for their speed, these typically had sharp vertical ends, a handling hole in the bow, and a flat-rimmed cockpit. Single-bladed paddles were sometimes used.

COPPER INUIT

They held the southern part of Banks Island, Victoria Island on both sides of Coronation Gulf, Bathurst Inlet, and Queen Maud Gulf, including among others the Kanghiryuarmiut on Banks Island, and the Kogloktogmiut or Kogluktomiut on the lower part of the Coppermine River. Their descendants live at Sachs Harbor, Holman, Cambridge Bay, Coppermine, Bathurst Inlet, and Umingmaktok.

GREENLAND INUIT (KALAALLIT)

Living chiefly on the western coast, including a northern section above Cape York on the Hayes Peninsula known as Polar Inuit, and an eastern group around Angmagssalik on the east coast.

IGLULIK INUIT

Held the western part of Baffin Island, and the Melville Peninsula south beyond Wager Bay almost to Chesterfield Inlet. They include the Tununmirmiut of Eclipse Sound, Tununirushirmiut of Admiralty Inlet, Aivillirmiut or Aivilingmiut on the Ross Welcome Sound and Melville Peninsula, and Sagdlirmiut or Sadlermiut on Southampton Island. Their present communities are at Arctic Bay, Pond Inlet on Baffin Island, Igloolik, Hall Beach, Repulse Bay, and Coral Harbor.

LABRADOR INUIT

Included groups extending from the Strait of Belle Isle along the coast of Labrador, Ungava Bay, Hudson Strait, and the east side of Hudson Bay as far south as Fort George. The most important groups were the Tahagmiut or Tarramiut of northern Quebec, Itivimiut of the east coast of Hudson Bay, and Kigiktagmiut or Qikirmiut of Belcher Islands. Their present communities are at Rigolet, Hopedale, Nain, Makkovik, Port Burwell, Port Chimo, Tasiujaq, Aupaluk, Koartac, Wakeham, Saglonc, Ivujivik, Akulivik, Povungnituk, Port Harrison, Sanikiluaq, and Poste-de-la-Baleine.

MACKENZIE INUIT

Groups around the delta of the Mackenzie River and Cape Bathurst. Their present groups live at Tuktoyaktuk, Paulatuk, Aklavik, and Inuvik, the latter two settlements shared with the Athabascan Kutchin.

NETSILIK INUIT

Settled west and south of the Gulf of Boothia. They include the Arveqtormiut or Arviqtuurmiut of Somerset Island, Netsilingmiut on the Boothia Peninsula, Utkuhikhalingmiut or Ukkusiksaligmiut on Back River, and Iluilermiut on Adelaide Peninsula and King William Island. Their settlements today are at Grise Fiord, Resolute, Spence Bay, Pelly Bay, and Gjoa Haven.

The Alaskan or Pacific (Yup'ik) Inuit groups can be divided as follows:

North Alaskan—from Point Barrow to Point Hope.

Northern Interior—to the south, on the Coville River, south to the Continental Divide.

Kotzebue—chiefly on Kotzebue Sound and the Kobuk River.

Bering Strait—located on Norton Sound.

There were a number of Inuit groups on the southern part of Norton Sound and the mouth of the Yukon River.

Kuskwogmiut—on the Kuskokwim River.

Nunivagmiut—on Nunivak Island.

Togiagmiut—on Togiak Bay and River.

Above: **An Inuit umiak. It is known in various forms, up to 40 feet (12 m) long, from Kodiak Island to Greenland. This open-topped cargo boat was sometimes used for walrus hunting and whaling, its wooden frame covered with sea, whale, or walrus hide. Up to a dozen crew could paddle, although sails (or more recently, outboard motors) might be installed.**

Below: **An Aleut hooded ceremonial parka or *kamleika*, a water-proof overdress made of sea mammal gut. The panel at the chin is dyed gut applique with red wool embroidery, while fur and dyed gut applique trim the cuffs and hem, and human hair decorates the seams. Worn by a person of high rank or by a shaman when making contact with the spirit world. Collected before 1869.**

Aglemiut—on the upper Alaska Peninsula.
Kaniag or Koniag—on Kodiak Island.
Chugach—on Prince William Sound.
Ugalakmiut—of Kayak Island.
Yuit or Yup'ik—of Cape Chukotsky, Siberia, and St.
    Lawrence Island.

The Alaskan groups today are:
North Alaskan at Barrow and Point Hope, in about
    six groups.
Northern Interior at Artaktuvuk Pass.
About twelve communities at Kotzebue, the largest
    being Kotzebue, Noatak, Selawik, and Noorvik.
Bering Strait, in about thirty small settlements, the
    largest at Nome, Shishmaref, Wales, Teller,
    White Mountain, St. Michael, Mountain,
    Koyuk, Unalakleet, and Shaktoolik.
The Yukon River delta area has about twenty
    groups including those south to Toksook Bay,
    the main ones at Kotlik, Alakanuk,
    Scammon Bay, Hooper Bay, Cheyak,
    Tanunak, Kipnuk.
The Kuskokwim River groups are at
    Kwigillingok, Eek, and Kwethluk, plus
    Togiamiut at Togiak, Clarks Point,
    and Dillingham.
On Nunivak Island are at Nash Harbor
    and Mekoryuk.
On St. Lawrence Island at Gambell
    and Savoonga.
On the upper Alaska Peninsula are about six
    communities including Chignik, Pilot Point,
    Egegik, and others.
On Kodiak Island are about ten groups,
    the largest at Kodiak.
Prince William Sound Inuit at Port Graham
    and Seward (much mixed with Athabascans).

In 1970, there was a total Inuit population for Alaska
of perhaps 25,000 or more. Canadian Inuit numbers
in 1970 were as follows:
Labrador groups number about 4,000.
Baffin Island, with groups at Pangnirtung, Frobisher

Below: **An Alaskan Inuit Wolf Dancer, c. 1915. He wears a wolf head mask, and seal skin dance mittens adorned with rattling puffin beaks.**

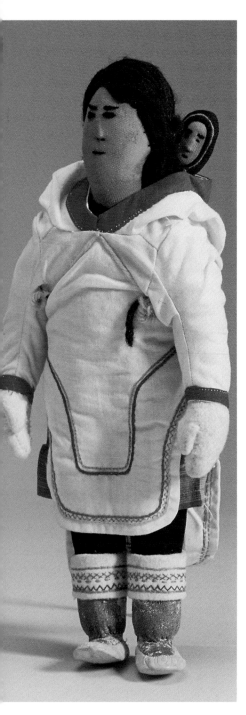

Above: **This cloth doll, made in the 1970s by a woman in the village of Hall Beach, Nunavut, wears seal skin *kamiit* (boots) and carries her child in the hood of her *amautik* (parka).**

Bay, and Lake Harbor, about 2,500.

Iglulik include 1,000 around Pond Inlet, 500 in the Chesterfield area, and 200 on Southampton Island.

Netsilik number perhaps 1,000 in the Spence Bay district. Caribou Inuit of the Chesterfield, Baker Lake, and Eskimo Point areas total some 2,000.

Copper Inuit of the Cambridge Bay and Coppermine areas, 1,500.

Mackenzie, about 1,500 in the Aklavik district.

The total 1970 population in Canada was thus over 20,000. The Greenland Inuits numbered about 13,500 in 1922.

The above is not a complete list; but a total recent population of over 70,000, including groups in Siberia, is probably correct. Census 2000 provides figures for the U.S. Inuit population—see box on page 29.

On April 1, 1999, the former Northwest Territories was divided in two, creating Nunavut, meaning "our land" in Inuktitut. The region is governed by the Inuit.

In many locations the remaining Inuits are hunters and, with a few exceptions (such as the Caribou Inuit), shore-dwelling sea hunters and wholly carnivorous. Traditionally skilled in making all the equipment necessary to catch all the food they required from the sea and its margins, they thrive in a climate and a terrain seemingly beyond the limits at which humans could survive. Their seal skin or caribou hide clothes, with the hair left on, were skillfully prepared and stitched to provide astonishing insulation against the cold; a person so dressed could sleep in the open at –22°F (–30°C). Their fitted tunic, called a *parka* in the west or *annuraaq* (anorak) in the east, was worn with trousers of polar bear or mole skin, and seal skin boots. In extreme cold, two layers of clothing were worn for added insulation, the inner layer with fur turned inward against the body and the outer layer with the fur to the outside.

Modern prefabricated bungalows with electric stoves and oil-fired furnaces are now known in all parts of the North. Today, the people of the central

Canadian Arctic live in this government-imposed Western-style housing, but for centuries they built structures from blocks of compacted snow, calling them *igdlu* or *aputiak*. Whether for a small family dwelling for a winter home, for a hunting-ground shelter, or for a giant community igloo built for drumming and dancing, the building method was the same.

Blocks of snow of the right density, each weighing approximately 18–26 pounds (8–12 kilograms), were cut using a snow knife. Each block of the first round of the igloo, placed onto the dimensions paced out on the snow-covered ground, was cut diagonally to begin shaping a spiral. The topmost round needed to be very carefully shaped and fitted so that the final keystone— a block with edges cut wider above than below—slotted neatly into place. Soft snow was packed into any cracks, with one or two left unfilled for ventilation, and a chimney, and windows with panes of sea-ice or translucent seal gut, were carved out. A porch would be added on to help keep cold drafts out of the living area and to provide storage for food, boots, and bulky outdoor clothing.

With heat from a seal-oil lamp and body heat from a few days' occupation of the igloo, the snow dome was transformed to one of solid ice, while the interior temperature was maintained at around 55°F (13°C). The family slept in the main room on a low platform covered in willow twigs and caribou furs.

Two types of water transport were known, the kayak in the east, and the umiak in the west. They also used a sled drawn by dog teams over ice or frozen mud. Today they may use a motorboat or snowmobile. Their principal food during the dark winter was seal, during the summer caribou; other sources of food were walrus, whale, musk ox, and wildfowl.

Two major rituals were celebrated annually: one to release the sea animals, and the other to welcome the sun's return, the herald of winter's end. In both events costumed figures, often masked and simultaneously male and female, suggest the renewal of creation. Shamans wore symbolically decorated attire.

A division of the Northern Wakashan family, who occupied the whole coast of British Columbia (except for the unrelated Bella Coola/Nuxalk), from Douglas Channel to Cape Mudge. They effectively formed a number of village tribelets which can be arranged dialectically as follows: starting in the north, the Haisla division included the Kitamaat on Douglas Channel and the Kitlope on Gardner Canal; the Heiltsuk division was the Heiltsuk (previously called Bella Bella) on Dean Channel and Milbanke Sound, China Hat or Haihais on Mussel Inlet, Somehulitk and Nohuntsitk on Wikeno Lake, and Wikeno or Oweekano on Rivers Inlet; and the Southern Kwakiutl were the Kwakiutl proper (Kwakwaka'wakw) of Smith Inlet, Kingcome Inlet, Gilford and Turnour Islands, Knight Inlet on the mainland, Hope Island (Nawiti), Alert Bay (Nimpkish), Klaskino Inlet (Koskimo), Quatsino and Fort Rupert (Kwawkewltk) on Vancouver Island.

The Kwakiutl were contacted by British and

U.S. coastal marine explorers during the late eighteenth century, but it was the establishment of the Hudson's Bay Company posts in the mid-nineteenth century which profoundly modified Kwakiutl culture, particularly among the northern groups. In 1780, the northern branches numbered 2,700 and the southern 4,500; but by 1906, they numbered only 852 and 1,257 respectively. In recent years, the Haisla and Heiltsuk numbered 848 (Kitamaat) and 1,245 (Bella Bella, Oweekano, etc.) respectively, and the Southern Kwakiutl 2,715 (Alert Bay, Fort Rupert, etc.). They are particularly known for their superb woodcarving and painting art, for totem poles, house gable fronts and columns, mortuary posts and masks. They also participated in the wealth display and distribution tradition known as the potlatch ceremony. In recent years, Alert Bay has seen a revival of Kwakwaka'wakw art and culture. The Campbell River and Cape Mudge bands presently considered Kwakwaka'wakw may have been at least in part Comox.

Opposite: **Kwakwaka'wakw Nation Crooked Beak Hamat'sa mask, carved by the Nimpkish artist Godfrey Bruce of Alert Bay. Kwakwaka'wakw tradition tells of supernatural beings who have existed since the beginning of time. Their continued presence is acknowledged in the Hamat'sa ceremony, performed even today as an element of a potlatch. Crooked Beak of Heaven, Galokwudzuwis, is one of three servant helpers of the Great Cannibal Spirit, Baxwbakwalanuksiwe. He makes his appearance in the third of four ritual dances whose purpose is to tame the Hamat'sa initiate who has been possessed by the spirit of Baxwbakwalanuksiwe.* In the course of the dances, the initiate becomes increasingly calm as his spirit is recaptured by his human family.**

*A video clip of a performance of this dance may be seen at www.coghlanart.com/video1.htm

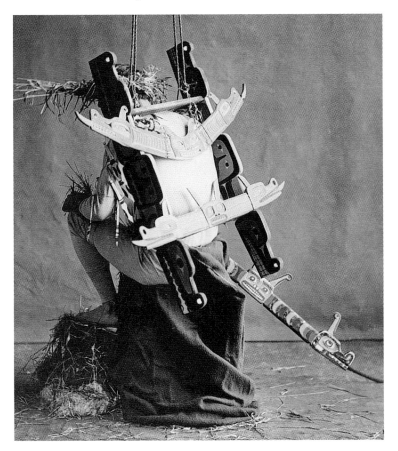

Left: **Kwakwaka'wakw (Southern Kwakiutl) war dancer with hoisting frame, photographed in 1904 by Charles H. Carpenter. Charles Nowell, who posed for this picture, was one of the last Kwakiutl dancers to be suspended by his pierced skin. The artifacts are now in the Field Museum, Chicago.**

An important Native people of the western shore of Vancouver Island, from Cape Cook in the north to beyond Barkley Sound. Although they had contact with European maritime explorers as early as 1592, Captain Cook gave the first accounts of these people in 1778. The settlement of the city of Victoria and the missionary work of the Roman Catholic Church gradually modified the traditional Nuu-chah-nulth culture. The Nuu-chah-nulth were both a sea and river people; they fished for halibut and cod, gathered kelp, and hunted whales, seals, and sea otters. They also gathered berries, fruits, and roots; they excelled in basketry, carving, and painting. An integral part of Northwest Coast culture, they are believed to have numbered 6,000 in 1780, slowly reduced to 2,159 by 1907. But by 1970, they had grown to 3,409, and by 1984 to 4,720. They have continued to occupy eighteen small village reserves on Vancouver Island, the main ones at Kyoquot, Ahousat, Clayoquot, Zeballos, Gold River, Nootka, Port Alberni (Tseshat), and Ucluelet.

Below: **The Vancouver Island Nuu-chah-nuth weavers Annie Williams and Emma George, photographed at the 1904 St. Louis Exposition where they demonstrated their expertise in basketry.**

MAKAH

A branch of the Nuu-chah-nulth (Nootka) located on Cape Flattery, Washington. Spanish, British, and American trading vessels contacted the Makah toward the end of the eighteenth century. Their economy was based upon the sea, and they hunted whales and seals. The Makah were party to an 1855 treaty that established their reservation on the tip of Cape Flattery within their former homeland. Their population was probably 2,000 in 1805, but smallpox lowered it to about 500 in 1850. They numbered 435 in 1905 and 919 in 1985. In 1992, 1,079 Makahs reportedly lived on their reservation. The figures provided by Census 200 were 2,488, including 483 of mixed descent.

OZETTE

Probably a subgroup of the Makah, occupying a village at the mouth of the Ozette River, Washington, south of their kinsmen. Sites around the village seem to have been occupied for several hundred years. In 1872, some 200 people lived there and at a small reservation established at Cape Alava in 1893. In the years since then, however, the Ozettes drifted away to other reservations, and by 1937 only one person remained. Recent archaeological excavations at the old village site have revealed the importance of whaling and other maritime pursuits to the Ozette. Various fine examples of material culture have also been found there.

Above: **Makah man, Neah Bay, Washington State, c. 1910, wearing a wolf mask and blanket decorated with buttons in totemic designs. Displayed in the foreground are other carved and painted masks typical of Northwest Coast tribes.**

Left: **Nuu-chah-nulth oil or grease dish with one end carved as the head of a wolf, the mouth set with otter teeth and a human astride its neck. At the other end of the dish is an unidentified creature. This piece would have been commissioned for the host of a potlatch.**

Below: **A Saulteaux woman, c. 1820. An early women's dress was the skin (later, trade cloth) slip supported over the shoulders by two straps to which a separate cape or sleeves were added in cold weather. This very loose garment required a belt tied at the back.**

By placing an *O* in front of *Chippewa* (O'chippewa), it can be seen that *Ojibwa* and *Chippewa* are merely different pronunciations of the same name. *Ojibwa* is used mostly in Canada, although *Saulteaux* is also used for the group west of Lake Winnipeg, while the term in the United States is *Chippewa*. The Ojibwa/Chippewa call themselves *Anishinabe*, meaning "original men." *Ojibwa*, or *Chippewa*, comes from the Algonkin word *otchipwa* meaning "to pucker," referring to the puckered seam of Ojibwa moccasins.

Although originally an Eastern Woodland people, the Ojibwa, like their northern cousins the Cree, were induced north and west by the early fur trade activities of the Hudson's Bay Company. From the 1670s onward, the Northern Ojibwa have occupied the interior of Ontario and the so-called Saulteaux—the areas about Lake Winnipeg, Lake Manitoba, and Lake Winnipegosis in present Manitoba and Lake of the Woods in western Ontario. They became dependent upon European trade goods which they secured in return for furs, at first from trading posts on James and Hudson Bays and later from interior posts. Their material culture became a mix of Native and European elements: they retained Native snares, birch bark canoes and toboggans, and birch bark, spruce, or hide dwellings; but they also adopted guns, commercial traps, canvas tents, log cabins, and lately outboard motors. Native dress also changed to a European style, though moccasins were still used until recently. Their Woodland traditions reveal themselves in the Midewiwin (Grand Medicine Society), vision quest, and certain forms of decorative art. The Ojibwa also seem to have had a belief in Kitchi-Manitou, a paramount beneficent force, a power in all natural things, and in the heroic trickster-transformer they call Nanabush. Many Saulteaux communities are now Christian, often Pentecostal.

Many Ojibwa have moved to urban Winnipeg, and they have suffered more than most through disruptive Euro-Canadian influences. Their early population in Canada is difficult or impossible to separate from that of other Ojibwa, but their descendants were reported to number about 30,000 in recent years. The Northern Ojibwa numbered 10,555 at Big Trout Lake, Caribou Lake, Fort Hope, Deer Lake, Osnaburgh, and other places in north central Ontario, plus Garden Hill, St. Theresa Point, and other locations in northeastern Manitoba. The so-called Saulteaux have thirty reserves around Lake Winnipeg, Lake of the Woods, and Lac Seul; the largest groups are Roseau River (sometimes given as Plains Ojibwa), Berens River, Fort Alexander, Peguis, Little Grand Rapids, Fairford, and Lake St. Martin in Manitoba; and Pikangikum, Islington, Grassy Narrows, Rat Portage, Whitefish Bay, La Seul, and other places in southwestern Ontario, numbering 18,869. In some locations Ojibwa speakers are called "Cree."

Right: **Kutchin baby belt, c.1890. Constructed of leather and velvet cloth and decorated with beadwork. The floral beadwork style of the Northern Athabascan Nations such as the Kutchin, shows one of many variations inspired by European influence which spread through much of North America during the 19th century.**

Below: **Cowichan/Halkomelem spirit dancer. An early representation of the Spirit Dance headdress originally made of hair, sometimes later of wool, and topped with feathers. Dancers used twirling movements hinting at the identity of the spirit power, usually an encounter with an animal in human form as a guardian spirit. This dance, still practiced by modern Coast Salish with initiation and dramatic ritual, is usually held in winter and is used as therapy for illness and alcohol or drug abuse.**

The coastal division of the Salishan family occupied coastal British Columbia from the Strait of Georgia south through Puget Sound in Washington, and south to the Siletz River in Oregon, except around the mouth of the Columbia River, which was occupied by the Chinook. There was one detached northern branch, the Nuxalk (Bella Coola) of Burke Channel, British Columbia. The Coast Salish lived in cedar plank houses facing rivers or the sea, and have a tradition of complex wood-carving art. Their dominant subsistence and material resources were salmon and red cedar, and they excelled in basketry and textiles.

CHEHALIS OR KWAIAILK

A number of groups on the Upper Chehalis River in Washington. A combined group of Kwaiailks, Lower Chehalis, and Chinook have occupied a small reservation at Oakville since 1864, with a population given as 382 in 1984, and 536 in Census 2000.

The Lower Chehalis was an important group on Washington's Chehalis River at the entrance to Grays Harbor. They do not exist today as an independent group. The Chehalis, with the Cowlitz and Quinault, form the Southwestern Coast Salish.

CLALLAM

The most numerous, warlike, and powerful group of Coast Salish, the Clallam are from Clallam County, Washington, below the Strait of Juan de Fuca. Their population before the epidemics of the early nineteenth century was between 2,000 and 3,000. After 1855, a few moved to the Skokomish Reservation, but most remained in Clallam County. They have a total recorded population of 1,200, with more descendants in the greater west coast area.

COMOX

At the northern end of the Strait of Georgia on both sides of Discovery Passage, centering on Cape Mudge, British Columbia. Their descendants are still connected with their former villages at Klahoose, Homalco, and

Sliammon, plus the Courtenay and Campbell River bands. They numbered 828 in recent years. The Seechelt and Pentlatch were very closely related, and are now called collectively "Northern Coast Salish."

COWICHAN OR HALKOMELEM

The mainland Cowichan occupied the lower Fraser River valley from Yale to Vancouver, British Columbia. By the end of the nineteenth century, around thirty small villages became reserves—the largest being Katzie, Chehalis, Cheam, Skwah, Soowahlie, Tzeachten, Seabird Island, and Musqueam. In recent years, the Cowichan numbered about 2,650, and 6,031 including the Island Halkomelem. The Island Cowichan occupied the southeastern coast of Vancouver Island, British Columbia, between the Comox to the north and the Songish to the south, including a number of islands. The name is also sometimes extended to the mainland Stalo or Fraser River Cowichan. There are six major Vancouver Cowichan groups—Chemainus, Cowichan, Halalt, Lyacksun, Malahat, and Penelakut. Their descendants numbered 2,184 in recent years.

COWLITZ

Several groups on the Cowlitz River, Lewis County, Washington. They probably numbered over 1,000 in the early nineteenth century. Decimated by epidemics in the 1850s, the Cowlitz merged with the Chehalis, Chinook, and Klickitats, with their descendants now at the Puyallup, Quinault, and Yakima reservations. Many still live in their ancestral homelands—Census 2000 reports 1,182, but other polls give the figure as 1,923.

DUWAMISH

On Puget Sound near Seattle. A few members moved to Port Madison, Muckleshoot, and other reservations, and a number survived in non-reservation areas. They have about 300 descendants.

LUMMI

Related to the Songish, they lived around Lummi and Bellingham Bays, Washington. In 1885, they moved to the Lummi Reservation. Census 2000 recorded 3,812

Above: **A masked "Sxwayxwey" dancer, who is a mainland-Halkomelem (Fraser River Cowichan), of British Columbia, Canada, c. 1920. These masks have characteristic eye protrusions and horns or ears usually carved in the form of a bird or beast. They are used in one class of public performance for persons undergoing life crises or changes in status, usually during potlatches. They are generally made from cedar and are most often attributed to the Central Coast Salish groups.**

Below: **A nineteenth-century Muckleshoot tumpline basket. Women of the Coast Salish tribes used baskets for collecting and storing fruit, vegetables, and shellfish, with large baskets supported by a tumpline across their foreheads. Baskets in the Cascades region were mainly coiled: stiff coils of cedar or spruce roots were decorated by covering them with strips of colored bear grass or cherry bark—a technique known as imbrication. Twined basketry was favored north and south of this region. This young Muckleshoot woman wears a rain-repellent cape and skirt of shredded cedar bark.**

Lummi or part Lummi. A small group, Swallah, on the San Juan Islands, was probably closely related.

MUCKLESHOOT
On the White River near Kent and Auburn, Washington. They were probably several minor groups who banded together after the Medicine Creek Treaty of 1854. The Muckleshoots numbered 194 in 1937, and 425 in 1984.

NANAIMO and SNONOWAS
Two small groups who belong with the Cowichan, on Vancouver Island near Nanaimo, British Columbia. There were 161 Nanaimos in 1907 and 525 in 1970. The Snonowas are now listed under the name Nanoose; they numbered 46 in 1907 and 86 in 1970.

NISQUALLY
A large group in forty villages on the Nisqually River, near Olympia, Washington. Most lived at the Nisqually Reservation—with a population of 62 in 1937 and 182 in 1984—a vast decline from their original numbers. The Nisqually, Squaxon, Steilacoom, Puyallup, Suquamish, and Snoqualmie are now collectively called "Southern Lushootseed." In 1990, the Nisqually were reported to number 390.

NOOKSACK
On the Nooksack River, Washington. After 1855, they were to move to the Lummi Reservation, but few did. Instead, they have lived independently around Everson, Nooksack, and Deming in Whatcom County, numbering 505 in 1970 and 1,168 in 1991.

NUXALK (BELLA COOLA)
Along the Burke Channel, British Columbia, surrounded by northern branches of the Kwakiutl, in particular the Heiltsuk. They have continued to occupy the village of Bella Coola, and were reported to number 311 in 1902, 334 in 1949, and 597 in 1970.

PUNTLATCH or PENTLATCH
A small Vancouver Island group near Qualicum, British Columbia, sometimes grouped with the Comox

or Cowichan. There were 42 people under the name Qualicum in recent years.

PUYALLUP
Related to the Nisqually, the Puyallup lived at the mouth of the Puyallup River and on Vashon Island near Tacoma, Washington. After the Medicine Creek Treaty they were principally located on the Puyallup Reservation near Tacoma. They were reported to number 322 in 1937 and 1,286 in 1984, but other groups have joined them over the years.

QUEETS OR QUAITSO
On the Queets River in Jefferson County, Washington. They moved to the Quinault Reservation after 1855 and are no longer reported separately. They probably have some 100 descendants.

QUINAULT
The largest Salishan group on Washington's Pacific shore, living mainly in the Quinault River valley and near Taholah. They remained fairly isolated until 1855 and the establishment of their reservation. From a group of about 1,000 in 1805, they diminished to a reported 196 in 1907 (probably a partial count), 1,293 in 1945, and 1,623 in 1984. Census 2000 recorded 2,377 Quinault and another 779 with partial ancestry.

SAMISH
Inhabiting various islands south of Bellingham Bay, in the Guemes Island area of Washington. A few joined the Lummi, but most have lived off the reservations around the Anacortes district. They have some 500 descendants.

SEECHELT
On the southern arms of Jervis Inlet, British Columbia, numbering 236 at their village in 1902, with a population of 471 in 1970, and 708 in 1987.

SILETZ
The southernmost Salish group on the river that bears their name, in Lincoln County, Oregon. Survivors were

Above: **A Nuxalk (Bella Coola) Indian wearing a mask dramatizing the supernatural being Echo. The dancer wears a cloth blanket that is decorated with trade buttons. The Bella Coola were an isolated Salishan tribe below Dean Channel, British Columbia, where their descendants still live. Photograph by Harlan I. Smith, c. 1910.**

Above: **Nuxalk (Bella Coola) dancers wearing masks and Chilkat blankets. Photographed in Berlin, Germany, c. 1885.**

TRIBAL RIGHTS AND BUSINESSES TODAY

Many tribes today have re-secured their land rights through skilled litigation. A number have reclaimed their tribal status in order to take advantage of non-tax and other dispensations previously accorded to them through treaty. These often include gaming rights, allowing a number of tribes to invest in gaming operations that enrich their communities. Profits often go toward building hospitals, schools, and cultural centers and creating jobs that improve the standard of living for both Indians and the areas in which they live.

Right: **Nuxalk (Bella Coola) dancers, brought to Germany by Norwegian ship's captain Adrian Jacobsen, performing a dance from the winter ceremonial cycle in Berlin, c. 1885.**

included on the Siletz Reservation as part of the much larger "Confederated Siletz" and are no longer reported separately.

SKAGIT, UPPER and LOWER

In Whatcom and Skagit Counties, Washington. The Lower Skagit have largely disappeared. Upper Skagit descendants live in Skagit County and number about 300. Another modern group, the Sauk-Suiattle, are also descendants of the Skagit River group and number about 260. The Kikiallus band at Mount Vernon and the Stillaguamish at Arlington and on the Arlington River can be included in this group. In 1992, the Upper Skagit numbered 552.

SNOHOMISH

At the mouth of the Snohomish River near Marysville and southern Whidbey Island, Washington. After 1855, they moved to the Snohomish Reservation, now called the Tulalip Reservation, where they numbered 1,099 in 1985 under the name "Tulalip."

SNOQUALMIE AND SKYKOMISH

Two closely related groups of the Snoqualmie and Tolt River basins. Some were included with the Snohomish at Tulalip. Most remained off reservations in their old territory and have about 500 descendants today.

SONGISH OR SANETCH OR STRAITS

On the southern coast of Vancouver Island, British Columbia, including adjacent islands. A number of Songish reserves still exist in their old territory— Tseycum, Beeche Bay, Panquachin, Tsawout, Esquimalt, Tsartlip, Sooke, and Songhees. Their population was about 1,130 in recent years.

SQUAMISH

At the northern end of Howe Sound and Burrard Inlet, mainland British Columbia, originally in many villages but restricted to six in 1909. In 1970, 1,143 were reported from Burrard Inlet and 1,089 from Squamish.

SQUAXON OR SQUAXIN

Related to the Nisqually, the Squaxon and the closely-connected Sahehwamish lived on Puget Sound between Hood Canal, Budd Inlet, and the Nisqually River. After 1854, a small reservation was established on Squaxon Island, but only a portion of these groups have lived there—given as 29 in 1949 and 302 in 1984. Together with the Lushootseed group and Twana they form the Southern Coast group of the Salishan family.

SEMIAHMOO

A small, apparently separate Salish band, probably closely related to the Songish and Lummi at the British Columbia and Washington State border, where 24 lived at a reserve bearing their name in recent years.

SUQUAMISH

Between Hood Canal and Puget Sound. The Port Madison Reservation was established for the Suquamish after 1855. Some 200 tribal members lived there in 1985, but many more lived in surrounding areas. In 1990, the Suquamish population was 780.

SWINOMISH

This group, closely related to the Skagit, occupied the mouth of the Skagit River and Whidbey Island. After 1855, most moved to the Swinomish Reservation. In 1985, they numbered 624, but a number of Skagit, Samish, Snohomish, Suquamish, and Duwamish have joined them over the years. The Swinomish, Skagit, Stillaguamish, and Snohomish are now collectively called "Northern Lushootseed."

TILLAMOOK

The Coast Salish domain was broken by the Chinook on the lower Columbia River, reappearing south of it in northwestern Oregon. The Tillamook, Nehalem, and Nestucca lived in Tillamook County, Oregon, and were the largest Coast Salish group south of the Columbia. Estimated at 2,200 in 1805, their numbers had fallen to 200 by 1900. The census of 1970 reported a population of 139 for the entire group.

CENSUS 2000

The numbers recorded for the Puget Sound Salish were:

Duwamish	166
Kikiallus	4
Muckleshoot	1,327
Nisqually	437
Nooksack	710
Port Madison	7
Puget Sound Salish	1
Puyallup	1,652
Samish	242
Sauk-Suiattle	114
Skokomish	706
Skykomish	5
Snohomish	484
Snoqualmie	301
Squaxin Island	594
Steilacoom	119
Stillaguamish	103
Suquamish	608
Swinomish	703
Tulalip	2,252
Upper Skagit	471
Total	11,034

A Northwest Coast nation along the southern coast of Alaska, between the northern part of British Columbia and the ocean. Although primarily dependent on the sea, the Tlingit were favorably situated to become highly successful traders, acting as middlemen between the interior Alaskan peoples and white traders. They were fine wood carvers and basket makers, and are renowned for their Chilkat blankets of mountain goat wool and cedar bark. Their basic political group was the village, divided into two *phratries*, or subdivisions, the Wolf and Raven totems. They lived in large community houses like most West Coast people and were dependent on the sea for food. Recent linguistic studies suggest that the Tlingit are related to the Athabascan groups and the Haida, together termed "Na-Dene."

The principal Tlingit subgroups were, north to south (but excluding the so-called Inland Tlingit, an Athabascan people), as follows: Yakutat (Yakutat Bay), Gonaho (mouth of Alsek River), Chilkat (Lynn Canal), Huna (Goss Sound), Auk (Stephens Passage), Taku (Taku River and Inlet), Hutsnuwu or Killisnoo (Admiralty Island), Sitka (Baranof and Chichagof Islands), Sumdum (Port Houghton), Kuiu (Kuiu Island), Kake (Kupreanof Island), Stikine (Stikine River), Henya (west coast Prince of Wales Island), Hehl (on Behm Canal), Sanya (Cape Fox), and Tongass (Portland Canal). They numbered some 10,000 in 1740; 6,763 in 1880; and 3,895 in 1950, but had recovered to about 7,000 by 1970 and 9,800 in 2000. Their main locations today are Yakutat, Klukwan, Juneau, Mount Edgecumbe, Sitka, Kake, Wrangell, Ketchikan, and Klawak.

INLAND TLINGIT

A group of Indians about Teslin village in southern Yukon and Atlin in northern British Columbia. Despite their name, some ethnographers believe them to be an Athabascan people, originally called Taku, who adopted Tlingit as their language owing

Below: **Tlingit, c. 1860.** Armor of heavy hide and wooden slats is worn with a heavy wooden helmet, with totemic crest, mounted on a wooden collar with eye and ventilation slits. The knife and club had blades of whale bone, trade iron, or copper, and crest images. Interclan wars to avenge injury or insult were sometimes settled by mock battles.

to extensive trade and intermarriage with the coastal Tlingit; others claim they were Tlingit who moved into the Taku Basin from the coast. Their material culture, including their dress, was a colorful mixture of coastal and interior traits, including the varied use of West Coast totemic decoration. They also held traditional-style potlatches until recently. In recent years, 250 lived at Teslin and 161 at Atlin.

TOTEM POLE MODELS

These were, and still are, made to satisfy the tourist market. Some models replicate full-sized poles, such as these (**Left**). The original was carved in 1890 by Tlingit carver William Ukas to honor a chief named Kohlteen. It was about 24 feet (7 m) tall and stood outside the Sun house at Killisnoo in the Stikine River region. This marine ivory model was made in the early years of the twentieth century. It was painted in red and black pigment, now mostly worn away. The top figure represents Kicks Bay mountain glacier on the Stikine River. Then comes Frog, emblem of the Kiks'adi people. Next is Old Raven, the Creator, and Young Raven, who made man. At the base of the pole is the Killisnoo Beaver, who was a chief's pet, with a small frog.

The other (**Right**) is a replica of the Chief Johnson or Kajuk totem pole, raised in Ketchikan, Alaska, in 1901 for the Ganaxadi Tlingit of the Raven moiety of the Tanta Kwan (Tongass) group. This model was made by Chief Johnson himself, purchased in 1901 by government agent Edgar Dewdney. A full-size replica of the original pole, carved by Israel Shotridge, was raised in 1989.

Below: **A spoon likely to have been painted, and probably also carved, by Tsimshian artist Freddie Alexcee, born at Port Simpson between 1853 and 1857. Alexcee's style fused a Western artistic painting tradition with Tsimshian carving.**

Bottom: **Tsimshian memorial ("totem") poles, c.. 1910, at Kitwanga on the Skeena River. Kitwanga is the home of the Gitksan tribe, who excelled at wood carving.**

This family is a combination of three closely related northern British Columbia groups: the Tsimshian proper on Alaska's lower Skeena River and Annette Island, the Niska or Nishga on the Nass River and neighboring coast, and the Gitksan or Kitksan on the upper Skeena River. As fisherman they caught salmon, codfish, and halibut; they hunted seals, sea lions, and whales. The interior bands hunted bears and deer and collected berries. Villages consisted of large wooden houses constructed of cedar planks, arranged in a row facing the sea or river; in front, canoes and boats were placed on runways or on the beach. Four *phratries*, or divisions—Raven, Wolf, Eagle, and Grizzly Bear—were distributed among the three groups. They were part of the strong art and carving tradition of the coastal people, and shared with the Tlingit and Haida the northern center of this remarkable culture.

The coastal Tsimshian were probably visited by Spanish, English, and U.S. explorers, and later, in the early nineteenth century, the Hudson's Bay Company established posts in Tsimshian territory. Their country was also overrun by miners during the Klondike Gold Rush of 1898. The Tsimshians have reserves in their old territory at Metlakatla (Alaska), Port Simpson, Kitselas (Tsimshian proper), Gitlakdamix, Canyon, Greenville, Kincolith (Niska), Kispaiox, Hazelton, Kitwancool, Kitwanga, and Kitsegukla (Kitksan). In 1780, the whole group numbered 5,500; in 1908, there were 1,840 Tsimshian; in 1906, there were 814 Niska; and in 1902, 1,120 Kitksan. In 1970, the same groups numbered 2,863, 2,364, and 2,503 respectively in British Columbia; and in 1950, there were 797 at New Metlakatla, Alaska. Census 2000 recorded 3,360 Tsimshian, including 1,183 with partial ancestry, and with the Metlakatla Indian Community figures given as 1,059 and 353 respectively.

ALEUT

Formed a divergent section of the Inuit or Eskimo family and were the original inhabitants of the long Aleutian Island chain and the Alaska Peninsula, in two general divisions. The Atka division held several of the outer islands as far as Attu Island and included parts of Agattu Island, Unalga Island in the Andreanof group, and Atka Island. The Unalaska division held the inner islands from Unalaska Island in the Fox group, Unimak Island, the Shumagin and Pribilof Islands, and the western Alaskan Peninsula, almost to Pilot Point. In the 1740s, they became known to the Russians, who cruelly mistreated and exploited them. Within a few decades their population was reduced from 16,000 to little more than 2,000.

The Aleuts developed extraordinary waterproof clothing, made from translucent seal gut, for use as raincoats or when at sea. During the early nineteenth century, the remaining Aleuts were converted by the Russian Orthodox Church, generally assumed some of the culture introduced by Europeans, and engaged in considerable intermarriage. In 1867, along with Alaska, they came under the control of the United States. In 1910, they were reported to number only 1,451, with many of mixed descent. Today small communities are still found, notably at Atka, on St. Pauls and St. George islands, at Unalaska, Akutan, King Cove, Belkofski, Sand Point, Port Noller, and a few other locations outside their former area, perhaps with a total population of 2,500.

BEOTHUK

The original inhabitants of the island of Newfoundland, perhaps contacted by Europeans as early as 1497 and subsequently known to explorers and fishermen. They were a river and bay people, living in conical tipis and using

CENSUS 2000

The numbers recorded for the Aleut were:

Aleut	6,606
Alutiq Aleut	319
Bristol Bay Aleut	610
Chugach Aleut	340
Koniag Aleut	1,457
Unangan Aleut	2,187

Below: **Haida Indians from Queen Charlotte Islands, in the late nineteenth century, wearing Chilkat blankets made of cedar bark twine and mountain goat wool. These blankets were called "Chilkats" as they were made by a Tlingit tribe of Southern Alaska who bore the same name. The men wear carved wooden headdress frontlets decorated with abalone shell and ermine fur.**

a very distinctively shaped bark canoe. They were known for annually painting their faces and bodies with red ocher as a means of tribal identity. Over the years, they were in constant dispute with invading French, English, and Micmac, and were often murdered at the slightest provocation. By the eighteenth century, they were restricted to Red Indian Lake and Exploits River. Their population was perhaps 450 in 1768, 72 in 1811, and only 14 in 1823. Shanawdithit or Nancy April, the last of her people, died in 1829. From the limited data available the Beothuk language appears to be an isolated family, although perhaps very distantly related to Algonkian.

CHILLUCKITTEQUAW

A Chinookan group of Hood River on the south side of the Columbia River in Oregon, and on the north side of the Columbia in Klickitat and Skamania Counties, Washington, along the White Salmon River. A few remained separate as late as 1895, mixed with a few Tenino (Waiam) at the Celilo Falls, Warm Springs, and Yakima reservations.

CHIMAKUM (CHEMAKUAN)

A small linguistic family formed by the grouping of the Chimakum proper, the Quileute, and the Hoh. The Chimakum proper may have been a Quileute subgroup who lived around the southern shores of the Strait of Juan de Fuca, Washington. They signed the Point-No-Point Treaty of 1855 but numbered less than 100 at that time. They joined the Twana at the Skokomish Reservation, where only three remained separate in 1890, and a few others merged with the Clallam. Census 2000 recorded only 3 Chemakuans.

Below: **A northern Northwest Coast painted wood Raven rattle, made in the early nineteenth century. This noble's dance rattle is carved in the form of Raven. A shaman lies on his back, his tongue connected to that of a kingfisher, while two frogs sit on the shaman's chest. The face of a hawk is on the underside. This rattle was held upside down when in use as shaking it right side up might cause the raven to fly away. The iconography of the raven rattle is believed to have originated with the Tlingit.**

COOS or KUSAN

A small language family formed by two groups in a narrow strip of the Oregon coast between the Coos and Coquille rivers. The northern division were the

Hanis or Coos proper, who lived around the bay and river that bear their name; the southern division were the Miluk on the Lower Coquille river near its estuary. Their combined population has been estimated at 2,000 in 1780. They had dugout canoes and took subsistence from the sea and gathered clams, camas roots, and berries. Some members of both groups were ultimately placed at the Siletz Reservation on the southern "Yachats" portion of the agency. In 1910, 93 were reported under the name "Kus;" in 1937, only 55; and 228 as "Kusa" in 1945. Today two reorganized groups who are the descendants of several groups, including Coos people who lost ancient lands around Coos Bay and on the old Yachats (Alsea) Reservation, Siletz agency, are petitioning the U.S. government for financial recompense. The number of people in 2000 with Coos ancestry is 211, plus an additional 163 with mixed ancestry. The Coos have been linked linguistically to the Siuslaw and Lower Umpqua (63 people in Census 2000) and with the other Alseans as the Oregon branch of the Penutian family.

Above: **A pair of late 20th-century Athabascan gauntlets, collected in British Columbia.**

Below: **A Tlingit Nation pendant amulet carved from a bear's tooth in the form of Wolf, the head tucked beneath the body and the tail curled. A perforation is drilled into the base of the tooth for suspension on a shaman's apron or collar. It was collected during the 1791-95 voyage of Captain George Vancouver.**

HOH

This group may have originally been a division of the Quileute people on Washington's Hoh River. A small reservation was established for the group in 1893 at the mouth of the Hoh River, where a few people have lived ever since. Census 2000 reports 124 members of the Hoh Indian Tribe under the Chimakum.

KALAPUYAN

A group of eight peoples speaking three languages, formerly living in Oregon's Willamette River valley. The Atfalati lived around Forest Grove in northwestern Oregon, and the Yamel above present McMinnville—the two forming one dialect division of the family. Farther south in Oregon were the Luckiamute on the river that bears their name, the Santiam around Lebanon, Chepenafa on Mary's River near Corvallis, Chelamela on

Long Tom Creek west of Eugene, and Calapooya near Eugene, all of whom spoke the central Kalapuyan dialect. Finally, above Oakland, Oregon, were the Yoncalla, who spoke the southern dialect. The Kalapuyans as a whole suffered greatly from the smallpox epidemics of 1782 and 1783. After coming into contact with white fur traders, they ultimately abandoned their Native economy and were unable to resist white encroachments into the Willamette Valley. Following treaties in 1851 and 1855, the surviving members of all the Kalapuyan moved to the Grand Ronde Reservation in Oregon, where their descendants are now organized as the "Confederated Tribes of the Grand Ronde Community of Oregon."

The census of 1910 reported 44 Atfalati, 5 Calapooya, 8 Luckiamute, 24 Chepenafa, 9 Santiam, 5 Yamel, and 11 Yoncalla; however, in 1930, the entire group was reported as 45 persons. At least twenty-four different groups were included in the Siletz–Grand Ronde complex, making it almost impossible for any one small group to preserve its identity. In 1955, 700 people were reported as descendants of the original groups of Grand Ronde Reservation. Just a year later, the reservation lost its recognition by the Bureau of Indian Affairs, and the federal government suspended its responsibility for any services and removed restrictions on their property. These services were partly restored in the 1970s, and in the 1980s the Grande Ronde reservation was reestablished and some original acreage restored. Census 2000 reported the Confederated Tribes of Grand Ronde at 2,130 plus 722 with partial ancestry

MONTAGNAIS-NASKAPI

The Algonkians of Quebec and Labrador from the St. Lawrence River north and west to James Bay. The Labrador and northern Quebec bands are sometimes given separate status as Naskapi (Nascapi). They belong

Above: **An Ojibwa style pouch or firebag of soft hide, still containing tinder, with floral designs in European glass beads on both sides. It was collected at Portage la Prairie, 65 miles (105 km) west of Winnipeg, and was probably made in the nineteenth century.**

to the Cree dialectic branch of the family, and the bands on the east coast of James Bay are now locally called East Main Cree or East Cree. They were skillful hunters using snares, traps, and bows, and when near the sea killed seals with harpoons. They fished with lines and bone hooks, and used wooden spears with bone points and light birch bark canoes. They did not farm, although they collected wild berries and roots, and hunted moose, caribou, and deer. Their clothing was made from caribou or moose hides and included coats, leggings, mittens, and fur robes with hoods attached. They had toboggans, portable conical lodges, and wigwams.

They ritualized their supernatural powers around good health and hunting, and a belief in a trickster-transformer figure. The Montagnais, a term used for most of the southern bands, were contacted by French explorer Samuel de Champlain in the early seventeenth century. Missionary and fur trade influences followed, but until fairly recently the northern bands have been quite remote from non-Native culture. Today, however, television, snowmobiles, prefabricated homes, and non-Native-run schools are found in most communities. In 1650, they perhaps numbered 5,500, gradually diminishing to 2,183 in 1906, but were reported as 11,697 in recent years. Their main southern (St. Lawrence) bands are at St-Augustin, Bersimis, Romaine, Mingan, Sept-Îles, Escoumains, and Natashquan; their interior bands at North West River (Labrador), Lac St-Jean, Mistassini, Nemaska, Waswanipi, and Chimo; and their James Bay bands are at Fort George, Eastmain, Rupert House, Paint Hills, and Great Whale River— these latter groups usually referred to as "East Main Cree." They were noted for the very fine linear and curving painted designs on their ceremonial dress, examples of which survive in museum collections in Europe and North America.

QUILEUTE or QUILLAYUTE
The principal group of the Chimakum family, at the mouth of the Quillayute River in Washington. The Pacific Ocean was their main source of subsistence, and they were proficient seal and whale hunters. They traded with U.S. and Russian seafarers beginning in 1792.

Above: **Stone and bone tools. The scraper or straight adze of iron, socketed into a carved length of bone or antler, is from British Columbia. The maul head with vertical and horizontal grooving and a flat face for a T-shaped handle, was excavated at Ogden Point, Victoria; and the adze head was found on Haida Gwaii (Queen Charlotte Islands).**

Refusing to move to the large Quinault Reservation, they were assigned their own reservation at La Push, Washington, in 1889. They numbered 383 in 1985; Census 2000 reported 466.

TAKELMA

A small linguistic family comprising two separate groups: the Takelma on the east side of the Klamath and Coast Mountains in the middle Rogue River area around Grants Pass, Oregon; and the Latgawa in the upper Rogue River area around Jacksonville, Oregon. Their houses were small brush shelters in summer and built of split sugar pine boards for winter. They decorated their clothing with dentalia shells, and tattooing was common. They also had cultural traits from California, and prized obsidian and Shasta basket hats. The Takelma resented intrusions on their lands and were involved in the so-called Rogue Wars of the 1850s. Afterwards, the U.S. Army decided to send the remaining Takelma and Latgawa to the Grand Ronde Reservation many miles to the north, where they arrived both overland and by sea. The Takelma probably numbered in excess of 1,000 in 1800, but later figures incorporated them in a mixed group known as "Upper Rogue River." Two groups of "Rogue River" were reported from Grand Ronde in 1937, numbering 58 and 46.

Above: **An Athabaskan "octopus bag" of trade cloth decorated with European glass beads. This form evolved from the earliest type of pouch made from whole animal skins, often worn folded over a belt. Pouches were originally made to carry tobacco or personal medicine. Collected before 1847.**

WASCO

A Chinookan group of the inland branch, their closest relatives being the Wishram, living near The Dalles on the Columbia River in Wasco County, Oregon. They were joined by the survivors of the Watlala and other tribes and removed to the Warm Springs Reservation, where a portion still remain as a separate people. In 1910, they numbered 242, 227 in 1937, and 260 in 1945. They are the only independently reported Chinook group today. The Dalles, Wasco, and Wascopan (219 reported in Census 2000) were divisions of this group.

WISHRAM
Probably the largest of the Chinookan groups, living farther up the Columbia River than any of their kinsmen. They lived principally in the present Klickitat County, Washington, and were closely related to the Wasco on the opposite (south) side of the Columbia. In 1800, they numbered about 1,000. In 1855, the remnants of the Wishram and a few other Chinook families were assigned to the Yakima Reservation. About 250 were incorporated with other groups on that reservation, and the 274 "Upper Chinook" reported in 1910 may have been this group. They are no longer reported separately from others of the Yakima nation.

YAKONAN or ALSEAN
A group on the Oregon coast forming a small linguistic family. From north to south these were the Yaquina on the Yaquina River near present Newport, the Alsea on the Alsea River, the Siuslaw on the Siuslaw River near Florence, and the Kuitsh or Lower Umpqua on the lower Umpqua River near Reedsport. The Siuslaw were the most linguistically divergent. They were coastal and river people—wealthy in dentalium shells and they hunted seals. They also held slaves. With a coastal location, they came into contact with white trading vessels in the late eighteenth century. In 1780, they perhaps numbered 5,000. The usual reductions followed, however, hastened by the activities of the Hudson's Bay Company, the influx of white miners, and the Rogue Wars of the 1850s. Survivors were moved to the Siletz Reservation on that part known as the Southern or Alsea Reservation. In 1910, a census reported only 29 Alsea, 19 Yaquina, and 7 Siuslaw; and in 1930, 9 Kuitsh. They are all now part of the so-called Confederated Siletz Indians of Oregon.

Below: **A nineteenth-century, northern-Northwest Coast portrait figure made of wood, with red and black pigment. A three-quarter or seated male figure is wearing a garment that has a high collar edged in red. The hairstyle and features are European. Such figures were often carved specifically for presentations that took place during potlatches.**

Acculturation. Cultural modification of an individual, group, or people by adapting or borrowing the cultural traits or social patterns of another group.

Agency. Represents the federal government on one or more Indian reservations under the Bureau of Indian Affairs (BIA), which is headed by a presidentially appointed commissioner. Many agencies, especially in the nineteenth century, were corrupt and often took financial advantage of the Indians they were supposed to manage and support.

Allotment. Legal process, c. 1880s–1930s, by which land on reservations not allocated to Indian families was made available to whites.

Anthropomorphic. Having the shape of, or having the characteristics of, humans; usually refers to an animal or god.

Appliqué. Decorative technique involving sewing down quills (usually porcupine) and seed beads onto hide or cloth using two threads, resulting in a flat mosaic surface.

Apron. Male apparel, front and back, which replaced the breechcloth for festive clothing during the nineteenth and twentieth centuries.

Bandolier bag. A prestige bag with a shoulder strap, usually with heavy beadwork, worn by men and sometimes women at tribal dances. Common among the Ojibwa and other Woodland groups.

Birch bark. Strong, thick bark used for canoes and various wigwam coverings. Used as well for a wide variety of containers that were also adapted for the European souvenir trade by the addition of colored porcupine quills, such as those produced by the Mi'kmaq and by the Ojibwa and Odawa of the Great Lakes area. Bark was an important resource, especially in the East, North and Northwest.

Buckskin. Hide leather from animals of the deer family—deer (white-tailed deer in the East, mule deer in the West), moose, or elk (wapiti)—used for clothing.

Less commonly used for dress were the hides of buffalo, bighorn sheep, Dall sheep, mountain goat, and caribou.

Bureau of Indian Affairs (BIA). Begun in 1824, transferred from the War Department to the Department of the Interior in 1849. Now, around half of the BIA's employees are Native American, and the Bureau provides services through its agencies in many big cities as well as on rural reservations.

Coiling. A method of making pottery in the American Southwest, in which walls of a vessel are built up by adding successive ropelike coils of clay.

Confederacy. A group of peoples or villages bound together politically or for defense (e.g., Iroquois, Creek).

Cradles. Any of three main devices used across the continent to transport or carry babies: the cradle board of the Woodland tribes (cloth or skin attached to a wooden board with a protecting angled bow), the baby-carrier of the Plains (a bag on a frame or triangular hood with a cloth base folded around the baby), and the flat elliptical board covered with skin or cloth, with a shallow bag or hide straps, of the Plateau.

Drum or Dream Dance. A variation of the Plains Grass Dance adopted by the Santee Sioux, Chippewa, and Menominee during the nineteenth century. Among these groups the movement had religious features that advocated friendship, even with whites.

Ethnographer. An anthropologist who studies and describes individual cultures.

Hairpipes. Tubular bone beads made by whites and traded to the Indians, often made up into vertical and horizontal rows called breastplates.

Housepost. Structural roof support for a Northwest Coast house, often carved with family or ancestral emblems.

Leggings. Male or female, covering ankle and leg to the knee or thigh (male), usually buckskin or cloth.

Medicine bundle. A group of objects, sometimes animal, bird, or mineral, etc., contained in a wrapping of buckskin or cloth, that gave access to considerable spiritual power when opened with the appropriate ritual. Mostly found among the eastern and Plains groups.

Moiety. A ceremonial division of a village, tribe, or nation.

Pan-Indian. Describes the modern mixed intertribal dances, costumes, powwows, and socializing leading to the reinforcement of ethnic and nationalist ties.

Parfleche. A rawhide envelope or box made to contain clothes or meat, often decorated with painted geometrical designs.

Peyote. A stimulant and hallucinogenic substance obtained from the peyote buttons of the mescal cactus.

Peyote Religion. The Native American Church, a part-Native and part-Christian religion originating in Mexico but developed among the Southern Plains tribes in Oklahoma, which has spread to many Native communities.

Powwow. Modern celebration, often intertribal and secular, held on most reservations throughout the year.

Prehistoric. In a Eurocentric view of American Indian archaeology, Indian life and its remains dated before A.D. 1492.

Rawhide. Usually hard, dehaired hide or skin used for parfleche cases, moccasin soles, shields, and drum-heads.

Reservation. Government-created lands to which Indian peoples were assigned, removed, or restricted during the nineteenth and twentieth centuries. In Canada they are called reserves.

Roach. A headdress of deer and porcupine hair, very popular for male war-dance attire, which originated among the eastern tribes and later spread among the Plains Indians along with the popular Omaha or Grass Dance,

the forerunner of the modern War and Straight dances.

Secularization of Missions. The 1834 breakup of California's Spanish missions, whereby Indians who had been forced to accept Catholicism and to labor at the missions were freed from service. Land that had been taken from the Indians was not returned as promised, however, but was instead distributed to Spanish settlers and other landowners.

Sinew. The tendon fiber from animals, used by Indians and Inuit as thread for sewing purposes.

Sweat lodge. A low, temporary, oval-shaped structure covered with skins or blankets, in which one sits in steam produced by splashing water on heated stones as a method of ritual purification.

Syllabics. A form of European-inspired writing consisting of syllabic characters used by the Cherokee in the nineteenth century and in other forms by the Cree and Inuit.

Termination. Withdrawal of U.S. government recognition of the protected status of, and services due to, an Indian reservation.

Tribe. A group of bands linked together genetically, politically, geographically, by religion, or by a common origin myth; a common language is the main reason. "Tribe" is itself a word that arouses controversy, with many prefering "Nation" or "People." Some "tribal" groups are only so described as a convenient tool for ethnographers studying collectively fragmented groups or collections of small groups of peoples who themselves recognized no such association.

War dance. Popular name for the secular male dances that developed in Oklahoma and other places after the spread of the Grass Dances from the eastern Plains-Prairie tribes, among whom it was connected with war societies. Many tribes had complex war and victory celebrations.

Weir. A brush or wood fence, or a net, set in a river to catch fish.

MUSEUMS

The United States naturally has the largest number of museums, with vast holdings of Indian material and art objects. The Peabody Museum of Archaeology and Ethnology at Harvard University, in Cambridge, Massachusetts, has over 500,000 ethnographic objects pertaining to North America, including a large number of Northwest Coast pieces. Many collections of Indian artifacts in major U.S. institutions were assembled by ethnologists and archaeologists who were working for, or contracted to, various major museums, such as Frank Speck and Frances Densmore for the Smithsonian Institution, Washington, D.C., or George Dorsey for the Field Museum of Natural History, Chicago.

Since the sixteenth century, the material culture of the Native peoples of North America has been collected and dispersed around the world. These objects, where they survived, often found their way into European museums, some founded in the eighteenth century. Unfortunately, these objects usually have missing or incomplete documentation, and because such material was collected during the European (British, French, Spanish, Russian) and later American exploration, exploitation, and colonization of North America, these collections may or may not accurately represent Native cultures. Collectors in the early days were usually sailors (Captain Cook), soldiers (Sir John Caldwell), Hudson's Bay Company agents, missionaries, traders, or explorers.

During the twentieth century, a number of museums have developed around the collections of private individuals. The most important was that of George Heye, whose museum was founded in 1916 (opened 1922) and located in New York City. It was called the Museum of the American Indian, Heye Foundation. This collection has now been incorporated into the National Museum of the American Indian, a huge building sited on the Mall in Washington, D.C., scheduled to open in September 2004. Other notable privately owned collections subsequently purchased or presented to scholarly institutions are the Haffenreffer Museum Collection at Brown University, Rhode Island; much of Milford G. Chandler's collection, which is now at the Detroit Institute of Arts; Adolph Spohr's collection at the Buffalo Bill Historical Center, Cody, Wyoming; and the impressive Arthur Speyer collection at the National Museums of Canada, Ottawa.

Many U.S. and Canadian museums and institutions have been active in publishing popular and scholarly ethnographic reports, including the Glenbow-Alberta Institute, the Royal Ontario Museum, Toronto, and, pre-eminently, the Smithsonian Institution, Washington, D.C. Most of the major U.S. museums have organized significant exhibitions of Indian art, and their accompanying catalogs and publications, often with Native input, contain important and valuable information.

In the recent past, a number of Indian-owned and -run museums have come into prominence, such as the Seneca-Iroquois National Museum, Salamanca, New York; the Turtle Museum at Niagara Falls; Woodland Cultural Centre, Brantford, Ontario, Canada; and the Pequot Museum, initiated with funding from the Pequots' successful gaming operation in Connecticut. The Pequots have also sponsored a number of Indian art exhibitions. Many smaller tribal museums are now found on a number of reservations across the United States.

There has also been much comment, debate, and honest disagreement between academics (Indian and non-Indian alike), museum personnel, and historians about the role of museums and the validity of ownership of Indian cultural material in what have been, in the past, non-Native institutions. Certain Indian groups have, through the legal process, won back from museums a number of funerary and religious objects, where these have been shown to be of major importance to living tribes or nations. The Native American Graves and Repatriation Act of 1990, now a federal law, has guided institutions to return artifacts to Native petitioners; some, such as the Field Museum of Chicago, while not strictly bound by this law, have voluntarily returned some remains and continue to negotiate loans and exhanges with various Native American groups. A listing of U.S. museums with Native American resources may be found at http://www.hanksville.org/NAresources/indices/NAmuseums.html.

FURTHER READING

Birchfield, D. L.(General Ed.): *The Encyclopedia of North American Indians,* Marshall Cavendish, 1997.

Brody, H.: *Maps and Dreams,* Jill Norman and Hobhouse Ltd, 1981.

Bruchac, Joseph: *Journal of Jesse Smoke: A Cherokee Boy: Trail of Tears, 1838.* Scholastic, Inc., 2001.

Buller, Laura: *Native Americans: An Inside Look at the Tribes and Traditions,* DK Publishing, Inc., 2001.

Coe, R. T.: *Sacred Circles: Two Thousand Years of North American Indian Art,* Arts Council of GB, 1976.

Cooper, Michael J.: *Indian School: Teaching the White Man's Way,* Houghton Mifflin Company, 1999.

Davis, M. B. (Ed.): *Native America in the Twentieth Century,* Garland Publishing, Inc., 1994.

Dennis, Y. W., Hischfelder, A. B., and Hirschfelder, Y: *Children of Native America Today,* Charlesbridge Publishing, Inc., 2003.

Despard, Yvone: *Folk Art Projects - North America,* Evan-Moor Educational Publishers, 1999.

Downs, D.: *Art of the Florida Seminole and Miccosukee Indians,* University Press of Florida, 1995.

Duncan, K. C.: *Northern Athapaskan Art: A Beadwork Tradition,* Un. Washington Press, 1984.

Ewers, J. C.: *Blackfeet Crafts,* "Indian Handicraft" series; Educational Division, U.S. Bureau of Indian Affairs, Haskell Institute, 1944.

Fenton, W. N.: *The False Faces of the Iroquois,* Un. Oklahoma Press, 1987.

Fleming, P. R., and Luskey, J.: *The North American Indians in Early Photographs,* Dorset Press, 1988.

Frazier, P.: *The Mohicans of Stockbridge,* Un. Nebraska Press, Lincoln, 1992.

Gidmark, D.: *Birchbark Canoe, Living Among the Algonquin,* Firefly Books, 1997.

Hail, B. A., and Duncan, K. C.: *Out of the North: The Subarctic Collection of the Haffenreffer Museum of Anthropology,* Brown University, 1989.

Harrison, J. D.: *Métis: People Between Two Worlds,* The Glentsaw-Alberta Institute in association with Douglas and McIntyre, 1985.

Hodge, F. (Ed.): *Handbook of American Indians North of Mexico,* two vols., BAEB 30; Smithsonian Institution, 1907–10.

Howard, J. H.: *Reprints in Anthropology Vol. 20:The Dakota or Sioux Indians,* J and L Reprint Co., 1980.

———: *Shawnee: The Ceremonialism of a Native American Tribe and its Cultural Background,* Ohio University Press, 1981.

Huck, B.: *Explaining the Fur Trade Routes of North America,* Heartland Press, 2000.

Johnson, M. J.: *Tribes of the Iroquois Confederacy,* "Men at Arms" series No. 395; Osprey Publishing, Ltd, 2003.

King, J. C. H.: *Thunderbird and Lightning: Indian Life in Northeastern North America 1600–1900,* British Museum Publications Ltd., 1982.

Lake-Thom, Bobby: *Spirits of the Earth: A Guide to Native American Symbols, Stories and Ceremonies,* Plume, 1997.

Lyford, C. A.: *The Crafts of the Ojibwa,* "Indian Handicrafts" series, U.S. BIA 1943.

Page, Jack: *In the Hands of the Great Spirit: The 20,000 Year History of American Indians,*The Free Press, 2003.

Paredes, J. A. (Ed.): *Indians of the Southwestern U.S. in the late 20th Century,* Un. Alabama Press, 1992.

Press, Petra, and Sita, Lisa: *Indians of the Northwest: Traditions, History, Legends and Life,* Gareth Stevens, 2000.

Rinaldi, Anne, *My Heart Is on the Ground: The Diary ol Nannie Little Rose, a Sioux Girl, Carlisle Indian School, Pennsylvania, 1880* (Dear American Series), Scholastic Inc., 1999.

Scriver, B.: *The Blackfeet: Artists of the Northern Plains,* The Lowell Press Inc., 1990.

Sita, Lisa: *Indians of the Northeast: Traditions, History, Legends and Life,* Gareth Stevens, 2000.

———: *Indians of the Great Plains: Traditions, History, Legends and Life,* Gareth Stevens, 2000.

———: *Indians of the Southwest: Traditions, History, Legends and Life,* Gareth Stevens, 2000.

Swanton, John R.: *Indian Tribes of the Lower Mississippi Valley and Adjacent Coast of the Gulf of Mexico;* BAEB 43; Smithsonian Institution, 1911.

Early History of the Creek Indians and Their Neighbors; BAEB 73; Smithsonian Institution, 1922.

———: *Indians of the Southeastern United States;* BAEB 137; Smithsonian Institution, 1946.

———: *The Indian Tribes of North America;* BAEB 145; Smithsonian Institution, 1952.

Waldman, Carl: *Atlas of The North American Indian,* Checkmark Books, 2000.

Wright, Muriel H.: *A Guide to the Indian Tribes of Oklahoma,* Un. Oklahoma Press, 1951.

INDEX OF TRIBES

This index cites references to all six volumes of the Native Tribes of North America set, using the following abbreviations for each of the books: GB = Great Basin and Plateau, NE = Northeast, NW = North and Northwest Coast, PP = Plains and Prairie, SE = Southeast, SW = California and the Southwest.

Abenaki: 9, 11, 25, 27, 48, 50, 51, 54, 56 (NE)

Abihka: 34 (SE)

Achomawi (Achumawi): 11, 50, 54 (SW)

Acolapissa: 11, 46, 47, 50 (SE)

Acoma Pueblo: 37, 42, 43, 44 (SW)

Adai: 11, 46, 51 (SE)

Ahtena: 11, 16, (NW)

Aivilingmiut (Aivillirmiut): 30 (NW)

Akokisa: 47 (SE)

Akudnirmiut: 29 (NW)

Alabama and Coushatta: 11, 12–13, 34, 39, 55 (SE)

Alaskan Inuit: 33 (NW)

Aleut: 9, 10, 11, 29, 30, 32, 51 (NW)

Algonkian (Algonquian): 24, 52, 54 (NW); 8, 16, 21, 42, 43, 50 (PP); 6, 8, 9, 10, 12, 13, 15, 25, 26, 27, 28, 29, 30, 32, 40, 41, 42, 47, 48, 50, 51, 52, 53, 54, 55, 56, 57 (NE)

Algonkian–Wakashan: 36 (NW)

Algonkin (Algonquin): 26, 40 (NW); 11, 48 (NE)

Alsea: 21, 53, 57 (NW)

Altamaha: 56–57 (SE)

Anadarko: 49–50 (SE)

Apache: 12, (NW); 42, 45 (GB); 9, 11, 12–21, 30, 44, 47, (SW); 8, 10, 26, 34, 38, 39, 54 (PP)

Apalachee: 11, 36, 39, 42, 46, 48 (SE)

Apalachicola: 48, 50 (SE)

Arapaho: 37, 45 (GB); 7, 8, 9, 10, 11, 12–13, 21, 22, 24, 41, 50 (PP); 48 (NE)

Arikara: 8, 11, 30, 36, 37, 49, 50 (PP)

Arkansea: see Quapaw

Assiniboine: 4, 11, 14,15, 25, 27, 28, 29, 40, 49, (PP)

Atakapa: 11, 26, 46–47, 56 (SE)

Atfalati: 53 (NW)

Athabascan (Athapascan or Athapaskan): 8, 9, 12–20, 25, 28, 31, 33, 41, 48, 53 (NW); 9, 11, 12, 13, 16, 17, 18, 30, 54 (SW); 34 (PP)

Atka: 51 (NW)

Atsina: see Gros Ventre

Atsugewi: see Achomawi

Attikamek: see Tête de Boule

Baffin Island Inuit: 29 (NW)

Bannock: 11, 33, 34, 38, 39, 50 (GB)

Bayogoula: 11, 46, 47 (SE)

Bear Lake: 8, 11 (NW)

Bear River: 13 (NW); 54 (NE)

Beaver: 11, 16, 19, 25 (NW); 38 (NE)

Beaver Hills People: 29 (PP)

Bella Coola: see Nuxalk

Beothuk: 8, 11, 51, 52 (NW)

Biloxi: 11, 47, 53, 54, 55, 56, (SE)

Blackfeet (Blackfoot): 13, 18, 22, 23, 26, 34, 36, 38, (GB); 7, 8, 9, 11, 14, 16-20, 25, 27, 29, 43, 50, 56 (PP)

Brotherton (Brothertown): 11, 13, 14, 26, 50, 52, 53, 54 (NE)

Bungi: see Plains Ojibwa

Caddo: see Kadohadacho

Caddoan: 16 (SW); 38, 50, 52, 56, 57 (PP); 23 (NE); 7, 39, 46, 49, 50–51, 52 (SE)

Cahto: see Kato

Cahuilla: 11, 50, 51, 53 (SW)

Calapooya: 54 (NW)

Calling River: 28 (PP)

Calusa: 11, 39, 47–48 (SE)

Cape Fear Indians: 11, 48 (SE)

Capinans: 47 (SE)

Caribou Inuit: 29, 34 (NW)

Carrier: 11, 16 (NW)

Cascade: see Watlala

Catawba: 11, 14–15, 32, 49 (SE)

Cathlamet: 11, 22 (NW)

Cathlapotle: 11, 23 (NW)

Cayuga: 11, 19, 22, 23, 24, 25, 38 (NE); 56 (SE)

Cayuse: 11, 26, 48, 50, 51, 53, 54, 57 (GB)

Chakchiuma: 11, 48, 50 (SE)

Chastacosta: 11, 12 (NW)

Chatot: 11, 48 (SE)

Chawanoke (Chowanoc): 54 (NE)

Chawasha: 26 (SE)

Chehalis: 11, 21, 22, 42, 43 (NW)

Chelamela: 53 (NW)

Chelan: 11, 51 (GB)

Chemakuan: see Chimakum

Chemehuevi: 31, 32, 33,34 (GB)

Chepenafa: 54 (NW)

Cheraw: 48–49 (SE)

Cherokee: 30 (SW); 8, 11, 14, 23, 49 (NE); 2, 8, 10, 11, 15, 16-23, 31, 32, 33, 36, 39, 41, 49, 51, 57 (SE)

Chetco: 11, 12, 14 (NW); 42 (PP)

Cheyenne: 42, 45 (GB); 7, 8, 10, 11, 12, 13, 21–24, 25, 41, 42, 51 (PP); 14, 48 (NE)

Chickamauga-Cherokee: 19 (SE)

Chickasaw: 8, 10, 11, 17, 24–25, 28, 29, 39, 41, 48, 51, 53 (SE)

Chilcotin: 11, 16–17, 18 (NW)

Chilluckittequaw: 11, 52 (NW)

Chilula and Whilkut: 11, 12 (NW)

Chimakum: 11, 52, 53, 55 (NW)

Chimariko: 11, 50 (SW)

Chinook: 7, 11, 21–23, 42, 43, 47, 52, 56, 57 (NW)

Chinookan: 23 (NW); 49, 57 (GB)

Chipewyan: 11, 25 (NW)

Chippewa: see Ojibwa

Chiricahua Apache: 11, 12–13 (SW)

Chitimacha: 11, 26–27, 32, 47, 54, 55 (SE)

Choctaw: 8, 10, 11, 24, 28–32, 36, 39, 41, 47, 48, 49, 52, 53, 54, 55 (SE)

Chugach (Chugachigniut): 10, 29, 51 (NW)

Chumash: 8, 11, 50–51 (SW)

Clackamas: 11, 23 (NW)

Clallam: 11, 42, 52 (NW)

Clatsop: 11, 22 (NW)

Clowwewalla: 11, 23 (NW)

Coast Rogue groups: 11, 12, 14–15 (NW)

Coast Salish: 7, 22, 23, 42–47 (NW); 12 (GB); 8 (PP)

Cochiti Pueblo: 37–38 (SW)

Cocopa (Cocopah): 11, 46, 47 (SW)

Coeur d'Alene: 11, 12, 26, 49, 50, 51 (GB)

Columbia: see Sinkiuse

Colville: 11, 29, 50, 51, 53, 54, 55, 57 (GB)

Comanche: 36, 39 (GB); 12, 14, 15, 16, 41 (SW); 7, 9, 10, 11, 12, 25–26, 34, 35, 53, 54 (PP)

Comox: 11, 37, 42, 43, 44 (NW)

Conoy: 11, 15, 50, 53 (NE)

Coos: 11, 13, 15, 52, 53 (NW)

Copper Inuit: 30, 34 (NW)

Coquille: 11, 13, 52, 53 (NW)

Costanoan: 7, 11 (SW)

Coushatta: see Alabama

Coweta: 34 (SE)

Cowichan: 42, 43 (NW)

Cowlitz: 11, 42, 43 (NW); 49, 52 (GB)
Cree: 11, 16, 19, 22, 24–26, 27, 55 (NW); 23 (GB); 8, 9, 10, 14, 15, 25, 27–29, 56 (PP); 18, 32, 37, 40, 48 (NE)
Cree–Assiniboine: 27 (PP)
Creek: see Muskogee
Cree-Métis: 19, 22, 26 (NW)
Croatoan: 54 (NE); 33 (SE)
Crow: 21 (NW); 8, 10, 26, 28, 34, 37, 38 (GB); 7, 9, 11, 22, 30–33, 42 (PP)
Crow Creek Sioux: 42 (PP)
Cupeño: 11, 50, 51, 53 (SW)
Cusabo: 11, 39, 49 (SE)

Dakota: see Sioux
Delaware: 11, 12–15, 48, 53, 57 (NE)
Dieguéno and Kamia: 11, 46–47 (SW)
Duwamish: 11, 43, 47 (NW)

Eastern Abenaki: 9, 50, 55 (NE)
Eastern Mono: 24, 25 (GB); 6 (SW)
Eastern Ojibwa, 25 (NE)
Eastern Shoshone (Wind River Shoshone): 36, 37, 38 (GB);
Eastern Siouan: 51, 52 (SE)
Entiat: see Wenatchee
Erie: 11, 24 (NE);
Eskimo: see Inuit
Eskimoan (Eskimoaleut): 29 (NW)
Esopus: 12, 26 (NE)
Esselen: 11, 51 (SW)
Eufaula: 34 (SE)
Eyak: 11, 17 (NW)

Five Nations: 16, 21, 30, 38 (NE); 17 (SE)
Flathead (Salish): 7, 21, 22, 23, 42–47 (NW); 9, 10, 11, 12–21, 22, 23, 50, 51, 52, 53, 54, 55, 56, 57 (GB); 15 (NE)
Fox: 24, 51 (NW); 39, 51, 52 (PP); 10, 11, 41, 42, 43,

44, 45, 46, 47, 48, 52 (NE)
Fresh Water Indians: 54 (SE)

Gabrieliño: 11, 51–52, 53 (SW)
Gatakas: 54 (PP)
Gosiute: 39, 41 (GB)
Great Lakes Indians: 25 (NW)
Greenland Inuit: 30, 31, 34 (NW)
Grigra: 55 (SE)
Gros Ventre: 7, 8, 11, 15, 16, 27, 50 (PP)
Guale: 49 (SE)

Haida: 6, 11, 12, 27–28, 48, 50, 51 (NW)
Haisla: 36, 37 (NW)
Haliwa: 54 (SE)
Halkomelem: see Cowichan
Han: 11, 17 (NW)
Hanis: 53 (NW)
Hasinai: 11, 46, 49–50, 51, 52 (SE)
Havasupai: 11, 47, 48 (SW)
Heiltsuk: 36, 37 (NW)
Hidatsa: 11, 30, 32, 33, 36, 50, 51 (PP)
Hitchiti: 11, 34, 39, 42, 50 (SE)
Ho Chunk: see Winnebago
Hoh: 11, 52, 53 (NW)
Hokan: 28, 50, 53, 54, 55 (SW)
Holikachuk: 17 (NW)
Holiwahali: 34 (SE)
Hoopa: see Hupa
Hopi Pueblos: 44–45 (SW)
Houma: 11, 46, 47, 48, 50 (SE)
House People: 28 (PP)
Hualapai: see Walapai
Huchnom: 57 (SW)
Hupa: 12, 13 (NW)
Huron: 4, 8, 11,16–18, 23, 24, 40, 41 (NE)

Iglulik Inuit: 30 (NW)
Illini: 40, 51, 52 (NE)
Illinois: see Illini
Ingalik: 11, 17, 18 (NW)
Inland Tlingit: 20, 48 (NW)
Inland/Interior Salish: 12, 13,

16, 17, 53, 54 (GB)
Inuit: 9, 10, 11, 17, 29–35 (NW)
Iowa: 11, 40, 51 (PP); 44, 46 (NE)
Ipai: see Diegueño
Iroquoian: 8, 16, 19, 22, 23, 25, 34, 39 (NE); 7, 17 (SE)
Iroquois: 26 (NW); 18 (GB); 40 (PP); cover, 8, 9, 10, 11, 12, 13, 15, 16, 19–25, 28, 30, 34, 38, 39, 46, 49, 50, 53, 55, 56, (NE); 15, 17, 31, 39, 47 (SE)
Isleta Pueblo: 38, 39 (SW)
Itivimiut: 30 (NW)

Jemez Pueblo: 39 (SW)
Jicarilla Apache: 11, 13–15, 16, 18, 21 (SW)
Juaneño: see Luiseño
Jumano: see Shuman

Kadohadacho (Caddo): 8, 50, 52, 56, 57 (PP); 7, 39, 46, 49, 50–51, 52 (SE)
Kalaallit: see Greenland Inuit
Kalapuyan: 11, 53–54 (NW)
Kalispel: 11, 12, 20, 51, 52 (GB)
Kamia: see Diegueño
Kanghiryuarmiut: 30 (NW)
Kaniag (Kaniagmiut): 10, 33 (NW)
Kansas: 11, 51, 52, 53 (PP); 41, (NE)
Karok (Karuk): 12–14 (NW); 7, 11, 49, 52, 53 (SW)
Kasihta: 34 (SE)
Kaska: 11, 17–18, 20 (NW)
Kaskaskia: 51 (NE)
Katapu: see Catawba
Kato: 11, 13 (NW)
Kaw: see Kansas
Kawaiisu: 11, 52 (SW)
Keyauwee: 11, 51 (SE)
Kichai: 11 (PP)
Kickapoo: 24, (NW); 10, 11, 40, 41, 47 (NE)
Kigiktagmiut: see Qikirmiut
Kiowa: 7, 9, 10, 11, 12, 25, 26, 34–35, 53, 54 (PP)
Kiowa Apache: 11, 12, 13,

15, 16 (SW); 10, 34, 54 (PP)
Kitanemuk: 11, 50, 52–53 (SW)
Kitsai: see Kichai
Klamath: 11, 35, 52, 53, 54 (GB); 13, 56, (NW)
Klickitat: 52, 53 (GB); 43, 52, (NW)
Koasati: see Alabama and Coushatta
Kogloktogmiut (Kogluktomiut): 30 (NW)
Kolchan: 11, 18 (NW)
Konkow: 23 (SW)
Kootenai (Kootenay): see Kutenai
Koroa: 55 (SE)
Kotzebue: 31 (NW)
Koyukon: 11, 18 (NW)
Kuitsch: see Umpqua
Kusan: see Coos
Kutchin: 11, 18, 31, 41 (NW)
Kutenai: 9, 10, 11, 20, 22–23 , 52 (GB)
Kwaiailk: see Chehalis
Kwakiutl: 6, 8, 10, 11, 36–37, 44, (NW)
Kwakwaka'wakw: see Kwakiutl
Kwalhioqua: 12 (NW)

Labrador Inuit: 30 (NW)
Laguna Pueblo: 39 (SW)
Lakes: see Senijextee
Lakota: see Teton Sioux
Lassik: 11, 15 (NW)
Latgawa: 56 (NW)
Lillooet: 11, 12, 52 (GB)
Lipan Apache (Tindi): 11, 16–17 (SW)
Lower Chehalis: 42 (NW)
Lower Chinook: 21–22 (NW)
Lower Connecticut River Tribes: 51 (NE)
Lower Housatonic River Tribes: see Paugusset
Lower Hudson River Tribes: see Wappinger
Lower Umpqua: 53, 57 (NW)
Luckiamute: 53, 54 (NW)
Luiseño and Juaneño: 11, 53 (SW)

Lumbee: 25, 54 (NE); 33, 53, 56 (SE)
Lummi: 11, 43–44, 45, 47 (NW)
Lushootseed: 47 (NW)
Lutuamian (Lutuami): 53 (GB)

Mackenzie Inuit: 31 (NW)
Mahican: 12, 13, 14, 15, 24, 26, 50, 52 (NE)
Maidu: 35 (GB); 7, 11, 22–23 (SW)
Makah: 11, 38–39 (NW)
Malecite: 11, 25, 27, 48, 54 (NE)
Maliseet: see Malecite
Manahoac: 11, 51 (SE)
Mandan: 8, 9, 11, 30, 32, 36–37, 40, 49, 50 (PP)
Maricopa: 11, 26, 27, 46, 47 (SW)
Mascouten: 11 (NE)
Massachuset: (Massachusett) 11, 51 (NE)
Mattaponi 57 (NE)
Matinecock: 12, 53 (NE)
Mattole: 11, 13 (NW)
Mdewakanton Sioux: 11, 45 (PP)
Meherrin: 23 (NE); 56 (SE)
Menominee (Menomini): 23, 53 (NE)
Mescalero Apache: 11, 13, 15, 16, 17–18 (SW)
Mesquakie: see Fox
Methow: 11, 53 (GB)
Métis: 27 (PP); 19 (NW)
Me-wuk: see Miwok
Miami: 11, 49, 51, 52 (NE)
Micmac: 52, (NW); 11, 25, 27, 28–29, 38, 48 (NE)
Mikasuki: 44, 45 (SE)
Miluk: 53 (NW)
Minitaree: see Hidatsa
Missisquoi: 50 (NE)
Missouri: 9, 11, 41, 51, 52, 53 (PP)
Miwok: 7, 11, 24–25 (SW)
Mobile: 11, 51–52 (SE)
Moctobi: 47 (SE)
Modoc: 11, 35, 52, 53, 54 (GB)

Mohave: 11, 46, 47–48 (SW)
Mohawk: 11, 19, 23, 24, 25, 30–31, 38, 56 (NE)
Mohegan: 11, 26, 48, 50, 52, 54, 56 (NE)
Mohican: see Mahican
Mojave: see Mohave
Molala: 11, 50, 54 (GB)
Monacan: 11, 52 (SE)
Monache: see Western Mono
Moneton: 11, 52 (SE)
Mono: 11, 24–25, 33, 35 (GB)
Montagnais-Naskapi: 26, 54–55 (NW); 48 (NE)
Montauk: 11, 48, 50, 53 (NE)
Muckleshoot: 11, 43, 44, 47 (NW)
Mugulasha: 47 (SE)
Multnomah: 11, 23 (NW)
Munsee: 12,14, 26, 35 (NE)
Muskogean: 7, 12, 24, 26, 28, 34, 39, 40, 42, 46, 48, 50, 51, 53, 54, 55, 56, 57 (SE)
Muskogee (Creek): 8, 35, 36, 49 (NE); 8, 10, 12, 17, 18, 28, 29, 32, 34–39, 41, 42, 43, 45, 46, 47, 49, 50, 57 (SE)

Na-Dene: 28, 48 (NW)
Nahyssan: 11, 52 (SE)
Nambe Pueblo: 39 (SW)
Nanaimo and Snonowas: 44 (NW)
Naniaba: 52 (SE)
Nansemond: 56 (SE)
Nanticoke: 11, 13, 15, 48, 50, 53, 57 (NE)
Napochi: 11, 46 (SE)
Narraganset: 11, 48, 50, 53, 56, 57 (NE)
Natchez: see Taensa
Natchitoches: 11, 46, 51, 52 (SE)
Nauset: 57 (NE)
Navajo: 12 (NW); 32, 45 (GB); 9, 11, 12, 17, 30–32, 34, 44 (SW); 32 (NE)
Nespelem: see Sanpoil
Nestucca: 47 (NW)

Netsilik Inuit: 31 (NW)
Netsilingmiut: 31 (NW)
Neutral: 11, 24 (NE)
Nez Perce: 21 (NW); 8, 10, 11, 26–30, 38, 51, 54, 57 (GB); 32 (PP); 15 (NE)
Niantic: 11, 53, 54 (NE)
Nicola: 11, 12, 18–19 (NW); 56 (GB)
Nipmuc (Nipmuck): 48, 54, 55, 56 (NE)
Nisenan: 22, 23 (SW)
Niska: 50 (NW)
Nisqually: 11, 44, 45, 47 (NW)
Nooksack: 11, 44, 47 (NW)
Nootka: see Nuu-chah-nulth
Norridgewock: 50 (NE)
North Carolina Algonkians: 54 (NE)
Northern Athabascan: 15–20, 41 (NW)
Northern Ojibwa: 25, 26, 40–41, 54 (NW); 37, 40, 48 (NE)
Northern Paiute: 24, 25, 31, 33, 34, 35, 50 (GB)
Northern Shoshone: 36, 37, 38, 39, 50 (GB)
Nottoway: 11, 23 (NE)
Ntlakyapmuk: see Thompson
Nugumiut: 29 (NW)
Nutka: see Nuu-chah-nulth
Nuu-chah-nulth: 5, 6, 10, 38–39 (NW)
Nuxalk: 11, 21, 36, 42, 45, 46 (NW)

Occaneechi: 11, 51, 52–53 (SE)
Oconee: 50 (SE)
Ofo: 11, 47, 53, 54, 55 (SE)
Ojibwa: 40–41 (NW); 8, 9, 10, 27, 28, 29, 40, 55 (PP); 8–11, 20, 32–37, 40, 41, 48, 54 (NE)
Okanagan: 53, 54, 55 (GB)
Okchai: 34 (SE)
Omaha: 8, 11, 39, 40, 45, 52, 53, 55 (PP)
Oneida: 11, 13, 19, 22, 23, 24, 26, 34, 38, 50 (NE)
Onondaga: 11, 19, 23, 24,

30, 38–39 (NE)
Opelousa: 47 (SE)
Oregon Penutian: 53 (NW)
Osage: 8, 11, 39, 40, 51, 52, 53 (PP)
Oto (Otoe): 8, 11, 40, 51, 52, 53, 54, 55 (PP)
Ottawa: 8, 11, 14, 17, 32, 36, 40, 41, 48, 49, 54 (NE)
Owens Valley Paiute: see Eastern Mono
Ozette: 11, 39 (NW)

Padlimiut: 29 (NW)
Padouca: 12 (SW)
Paiute: 11, 24, 25, 31–35, 37, 39, 40, 42, 43, 50. 52, 56 (GB); 6 (SW)
Pakana: 34 (SE)
Palouse: 11, 48, 53, 54 (GB)
Pamunkey: 57 (NE)
Panamint: 24, 25, 39, 41 (GB)
Papago: see Pima
Parklands People: 28 (PP)
Pascagoula: 11, 53 (SE)
Passamaquoddy: 11, 25, 27, 48, 50, 54, 55 (NE)
Patwin: 8, 56 (SW)
Paugusset: 55 (NE)
Pawnee: 8, 9, 10, 11, 12, 22, 38–39, 48, 50, 52 (PP); 15, 44 (NE)
Pawokti: 12 (SE)
Pawtucket (Pawtuxet): see Pennacook
Pecos Pueblo: 11, 34 (SW)
Pedee: 11, 53 (SE)
Pennacook (Pawtucket): 50, 51, 55 (NE)
Penobscot: 27, 50, 51 (NE)
Pensacola: 11, 53 (SE)
Pentlatch: see Puntlatch
Penutian: 26 (GB); 7, 22, 24, 56 (SW)
Peoria: 51, 52 (NE)
Pequawket: see Pigwacket
Pequot: 11, 43, 48, 50, 52, 55, 56 (NE)
Petun: 11, 16, 23 (NE)
Piankashaw: 52 (NE)
Picuris Pueblo: 40 (SW)

Piegan: 16, 18, 20 (PP)
Pigwacket: 50 (NE)
Pikuni: see Piegan
Pima and Papago: 9, 10, 11, 26–27, 46, 47 (SW)
Piscataway: see Conoy
Pit River: 35 (GB); 29, 50 (SW)
Plains Cree: 10, 25, 27–29 (PP)
Plains Ojibwa: 41 (NW); 9, 27, 28, 29, 55 (PP); 32 (NE)
Pocomoke: 56 (SE)
Pocomtuc (Pocumtuck): 48, 54, 56 (NE)
Podunk: 51 (NE)
Pojoaque Pueblo: 40 (SW)
Pokanoket: see Wampanoag
Pomo: 7, 8, 11, 23, 28–29, 55 (SW)
Ponca: 8, 11, 39, 40, 53, 55 (PP)
Potawatomi: 11, 40–41 (NE)
Powhatan: 11, 48, 56, 57 (NE)
Pueblo Dwellers: 33–45 (SW); 9, 34, 38, 54 (PP)
Puntlatch: 43, 44–45 (NW)
Puyallup: 11, 43, 44, 45, 47 (NW)

Qikirmiut: 30 (NW)
Quaitso: see Queets
Quapaw 53, 55, 56 (PP); 17 (NE)
Quechan: see Yuma
Queets: 45 (NW)
Quileute (Quillayute): 11, 52, 53, 55–56 (NW)
Quinault: 11, 21, 22, 42, 43, 45, 56 (NW)
Quinnipiac: 51 (NE)
Quiripi: 48, 51 (NE)

Rabbitskins: 28 (PP)
Rappahannock: 57 (NE)
Raritan: 12, 50 (NE)
Ree: see Arikara
River People: 26 (SW); 29 (PP)
Rocky Boy and United States Cree: 29 (PP)

Sac: see Fox
Sadlermiut: 30 (NW)
Sagdlir Miut: see Sadlermiut
Sahaptian (Shahaptian): 11, 26, 48, 54, 56 (GB); 8 (PP)
Sakonnet: 57 (NE)
Salina (Salinan): 53 (SW)
Salish: see Flathead
Salishan: 22, 23, 42, 45, 47, (NW); 10, 12, 50, 51, 52, 54, 55, 56, 57 (GB)
Samish: 11, 45, 47 (NW)
San Felipe Pueblo: 40 (SW)
San Ildefonso Pueblo: 40–41, 43 (SW)
San Juan Pueblo: 41 (SW)
Sandia Pueblo: 41 (SW)
Sanetch: see Songish
Sanpoil: 11, 51, 54 (GB)
Santa Ana Pueblo: 42 (SW)
Santa Clara Pueblo: front cover, 10, 34, 36, 42, 44 (SW)
Santee Sioux: 43, 45 (PP)
Santiam: 54 (NW); 53 (GB)
Santo Domingo Pueblo: 42 (SW)
Saponi: 11, 51, 52, 53, 54 (SE)
Sara: see Cheraw
Sarsi (Sarcee): 11, 29, 56, 57 (PP)
Sauk: see Fox
Saulteaux: 25, 26, 40, 41 (NW); 27, 55 (PP); 32, 36 (NE)
Seechelt: 43, 45 (NW)
Sekani: 11, 19 (NW)
Semiahmoo: 11, 47 (NW)
Seminole: 8, 10, 11, 18, 34, 35, 39, 42–45, 46, 48, 49, 50, 53, 54, 57 (SE)
Seneca: front cover, 2, 14, 19, 22, 23, 24, 25, 38, 39, 49 (NE)
Senijextee: 51 (GB)
Serrano: 11, 50, 52, 53–54, 55 (SW)
Shahaptian: see Sahaptian
Shasta: 56 (NW); 7, 11, 54 (SW)
Shawnee: 24, (NW); 11, 14, 48–49, 59 (NE); 15, 19,

34 (SE)
Shinnecock: 53 (NE)
Shoshone: 6, 11, 26, 31, 35, 36–41, 43, 45, 50 (GB); 7, 8, 9, 12, 16, 22, 25, 26, 32 (PP)
Shoshonean: 6, 25, 31, 37, 39, 42 (GB); 33, 44 (SW); 25 (PP)
Shuman: 56 (PP)
Shuswap: 11, 12, 22, 52, 55 (GB)
Sia Pueblo: see Zia
Sikosuilarmiut: 29 (NW)
Siletz: 11, 12, 13, 14, 15, 45–46, 53, 54, 57 (NW); 54 (SW)
Sinkaietk: see Okanagan
Sinkiuse: 11, 50, 51, 53, 55 (GB)
Sinkyone: 11, 14 (NW)
Siouan: 8, 14, 30, 36, 40, 50, 51, 52, 53, 54, 55 (PP); 57 (NE); 7, 14, 47, 49, 51, 52, 53, 56 (SE)
Sioux: 28, 35, (GB); 8, 9, 10, 11, 21, 22, 23, 33, 34, 40–49 (PP); 32 (NE)
Sisseton Sioux: 11, 42, 43, 45 (PP)
Sissipahaw: 11, 49, 54 (SE)
Siuslaw: 53, 57 (NW)
Skagit, Upper and Lower: 11, 46, 47 (NW)
Skilloot: 11, 23 (NW)
Skitswish: see Coeur d'Alene
Skokomish: see Snoqualmie
Skykomish: see Snoqualmie
Smith River: see Tolowa
Snake: 16 (PP)
Snohomish: 11, 46, 47 (NW)
Snonowas: see Nanaimo
Snoqualmie: 11, 42, 44, 46, 47, 52 (NW)
Songish: 43, 46, 47 (NW)
Southern Paiute: 31, 32, 33, 34, 35, 42, 43 (GB)
Spokan (Spokane): 11, 12, 20, 26, 50, 51, 54, 55, 56 (GB)
Squamish: 11, 46 (NW)
Squaxon (Squaxin): 47 (NW)

Stalo: 11, 43 (NW)
Stillaguamish: 47 (NW)
Stockbridge: 11, 14, 26, 57 (NE)
Stoney: see Assiniboine
Straits: see Songish
Summerville: 41, 48, 49 (SE)
Suquamish: 11, 44, 47 (NW)
Susquehannock: 11, 23, 50, 56 (NE)
Swampy Cree: see West Main Cree
Swinomish: 11, 47 (NW)

Taensa (Natchez): 6, 11, 27, 29, 39, 40–41, 54, 55 (SE)
Tagish: 11, 17, 20 (NW)
Tahagmiut: 30 (NW)
Tahltan: 11, 17, 20 (NW)
Takelma: 11, 56 (NW)
Taltushtuntude: 11, 14 (NW)
Tamali (Tamathli): 50 (SE)
Tanacross: 19 (NW)
Tanaina: 11, 19–20 (NW)
Tanana: 11, 18, 19 (NW)
Taos Pueblo: 8, 38, 42–43, 45 (SW)
Tarramiut: see Tahagmiut
Tawakoni: 11, 57 (PP)
Tenino: 52 (NW); 11, 54, 56 (GB)
Tesuque Pueblo: 40, 43 (SW)
Tête de Boule: 11, 26 (NW)
Teton Sioux: 11, 41, 43, 45 (PP)
Thompson: 19 (NW); 56 (GB)
Tillamook: 11, 47 (NW)
Timucua: 54–55 (SE)
Tinde: see Jicarilla Apache
Tionontati: see Petun
Tiou: 55 (SE)
Tipai: see Diegueño
Tlingit: 6, 10, 11, 12, 17, 19, 20, 28, 48–49, 50, 51, 52, 53 (NW)
Tobacco Nation: see Petun
Tohome: 52 (SE)
Tolowa: 12, 14, 15 (NW)
Tonkawa: 11, 16 (SW)
Touchwood Hills: 28 (PP)
Tsimshian: 6, 11, 28, 50 (NW)

Tsuu Tina: see Sarsi
Tubatulabal: 11, 52, 54–55 (SW)
Tulsa: 34 (SE)
Tunica: 11, 26, 39, 47, 54, 55, 56, 57 (SE)
Tunican: 26, 39, 55 (SE)
Tununirushirmiut: 30 (NW)
Tunxis: 51 (NE)
Tuscarora: 11, 23, 24, 25, 30, 38, 39 (NE); 15, 33 (SE)
Tuskegee: 11, 39, 55–56 (SE)
Tutchone: 11, 20 (NW)
Tutelo: 11, 51, 52, 53, 56 (SE); 40 (PP)
Tututni: see Coast Rogue groups
Twana: see Snoqualmie

Ukkusiksaligmiut: 31 (NW)
Umatilla: 8, 10, 11, 26, 48, 50, 56, 57 (GB)
Umpqua: 11, 15, 53, 57 (NW)
Unalaska: 51 (NW)
Unami: 12, 14 (NE); 57 (SE)
United States Cree: see Rocky Boy
Unquachog: 48 (NE)
Upper Chinook: 22, 23, 57 (NW)
Upper Kwaiailk: see Chehalis
Upper Umpqua: 15 (NW)
Ute: 11, 31, 32, 37, 40, 42–47 (GB); 12 (PP)
Utina: see Timucua

Utkuhikhalingmiut: see Ukkusiksaligmiut
Uto-Aztecan: 26, 51, 52, 54 (SW); 56 (PP)

Vanyume: 53 (SW)

Waccamaw: 11, 53, 56 (SE)
Waco: 11, 57 (PP)
Wahpekute Sioux: 11, 46, 47 (PP)
Wahpeton Sioux: 11, 45, 47 (PP)
Waiilatpuan: 11, 50, 53 (GB)
Wailaki: 11, 15 (NW)
Wakashan: 36 (NW)
Wakiakum: 22 (NW)
Wakokai: 34 (SE)
Walapai: 11, 47, 48 (SW)
Walla Walla: 11, 26, 48, 50, 57 (GB)
Walula: see Walla Walla
Wampanoag: 57 (NE)
Wangunk: 51 (NE)
Wappato: see Multnomah
Wappinger and Lower Hudson River Tribes: 12, 26, 51, 57 (NE)
Wappo: 11, 55, 57 (SW)
Wasco: 11, 21, 22, 23, 56–57 (NW); 49, 57 (GB)
Washa: 26, 27 (SE)
Washoe (Washo): 11, 55 (SW)
Wateree: 11, 56 (SE)
Watlala: 11, 23, 56 (NW)
Wawyachtonok: see

Weantinock
Wea: 52 (NE)
Weantinock: 55 (NE)
Wenatchee (Wenatchi): 11, 12, 50, 51, 55, 57 (GB)
West Main Cree: 24–25 (NW); 27, 28, 29 (PP); 37 (NE)
Western Abenaki: 11, 50, 55 (NE)
Western Apache: 12, 14, 18–21, 30, (SW)
Western Mono (Monache): 25 (GB)
Western Shoshone: 37, 39, 40. 41, 43 (GB)
Western Woods Cree: 25–26 (NW)
Westo: 57 (SE)
Whilkut: see Chilula
Wichita: 8, 11, 25, 52, 56, 57 (PP); 14 (NE); 51 (SE)
Wicomiss: 53 (NE)
Willapa: 22 (NW)
Wind River Shoshone: see Eastern Shoshone
Winnebago: 36, 40,51,52, 53, 54 (PP); 56, 57 (NE)
Wintun (Wintu): 15 (NW); 7, 11, 55–56, 57 (SW)
Winyaw: 56 (SE)
Wishram: 11, 22, 23, 56, 57 (NW); 49, 57 (GB)
Wiyot: 11, 49, 56 (SW)
Woccon: 56 (SE)
Wyandot: see Huron

Yadkin: 49 (SE)
Yahi: 56, 57 (SW)
Yakama: see Yakima
Yakima: 43, 52 (NW); 10, 11, 26, 48–49, 52, 54, 56, 57 (GB)
Yakonan: see Alsea
Yamasee: 11, 15, 36, 39, 42, 54, 56–57 (SE)
Yamasee-Cusabo: 39 (SE)
Yamel: 53 (NW)
Yana: 7, 11, 56 (SW)
Yankton Sioux: 11, 41, 45, 48 (PP)
Yanktonai Sioux: 11, 14, 15, 41, 45 (PP)
Yaquina: 57 (NW)
Yatasi: 52 (SE)
Yavapai: 11, 47, 48 (SW)
Yokuts: 25 (GB); 7, 11, 52, 56–57 (SW)
Yuchi: 48 (NE); 11, 34, 39, 46, 57 (SE)
Yuit: 33 (NW)
Yuki: 11, 55, 57 (SW)
Yuma: 11, 46, 47, 48 (SW)
Yuman Tribes: 26, 46–48 (SW)
Yurok: 12, 14 (NW); 11, 48, 49, 52, 56 (SW)

Zia or Sia Pueblo: 11, 33, 43 (SW)
Zuñi: 8, 10, 11, 30, 33, 34, 37, 43–44 (SW)

ABOUT THE CONTRIBUTORS

Jane Burkinshaw (Contributing Author)
The Assistant Curator of Ethnography of the Royal Albert Memorial Museum in Exeter, Devon, England, Burkinshaw is the author of *Klaya-Ho-Alth* ("Welcome"), an introduction to the Royal Albert Museum's collections from the Northwest Coast of North America.

Richard Hook (Illustrator and Contributing Author
An internationally respected professional illustrator specializing in historical and anthropological subjects for more than thirty years, Hook has had a lifelong interest in Native American culture that has inspired his remarkable artwork. He has been widely published in the United States, Europe, and Japan. A lifelong interest in Native

American culture led to his selection as illustrator for the Denali Press Award-winning *The Encyclopedia of Native American Tribes*.

Michael G. Johnson (Author)
Johnson has researched the material culture, demography, and linguistic relationships of Native American peoples for more than thirty years, through

academic institutions in North America and Europe and during numerous field studies conducted with the cooperation and hospitality of many Native American communities. He has published a number of books, in particular the Denali Press Award-winning *Encyclopedia of Native American Tribes*.